# *Boadicea*

---

# Contents

# BOADICEA

# BOADICEA.

## ACT I.

SCENE I.—In the cale of Langotham, in Wales.—Scenery rough and romantic, purely Welch. Enter Comos and his band.—Comos retires apart from the body, while they pass in review before him.

*Comos.* c. Halt! Then ye arc what these foreign lords would model into greatness ! Be there such thought among ye of this high position? Which of ye, think, be the best sample for the work ? for they would make gods of ye! [They look at each other, but say nothing.] Aye, there is much wisdom in that silent lip, and self-denial! Yet, methinks ye are deceived, for I hold no heart in a flattering homage: they please ye but for plunder and rapine! Be cautious to adversity. Pride, like power, betrays the poor! Let hope be, battle brave with this adversity! Pass on and form upon shore of Bumairs. I'll meet thee there, anon. [***All exit. About to go.***] Ah, here comes our friends Panics and Garbolos! Welcome, Chiefs; welcome, Garbolos!

*Garbolos.* Welcome, Comos.

*Comos.* And you, Paulos.

*Paulos.* Welcome!

*Comos.* And what, so down at lip, and still, reserved ? remorse!—

*Garbolos.* Disturb him not, good Comos!

*Comos.* But it ill becomes one of the Brigantes' Chiefs to be so over sad !

*Paulos.* Aye, sad and sorry!

*Comos.* How ?

*Paulos.* For ever since I first knew myself, and learned to reason with the things of life, I have held superstition in much good esteem!

*Comos.* Ha, ha, ha!

*Paulos.* What, mock me, Comos !

*Comos.* No; but I did think a Chief so handled in this world of times as you have been, Paulos, would long ago have shut thy mind 'gainst childish fears.

*Paulos.* Fear never did possess me ! But when I see events to come, I reckon on their consequences, from every sign !

*Comos*. Why, what have ye seen, so wondrous ?

*Paulos.* On yester eve, as from my door I looked out upon the dingy sky, for some bright spot to fasten hope unto, the new made satellite that shot up quickly from behind the wood, fell on my nearer shoulder.

*Comos.* Well!

*Paulos.* Which doth predict, from many such which I have seen, that we have no better fate stored here, while she holds on her sway!

*Comos.* Is this all ?

*Paulos.* Yes.

*Comos.* Then I should truly laugh at thee. Why, Paulos ! What think you of this, Garbolos? Ha, ha, ha!

*Garbolos.* Ah. it is Paulos, even to life.

*Comos.* Away, Paulos, with such fear. I'll show thee a satellite, ere another sign shall come that shall shine brighter on thy off shoulder, and make thee a lion, not a lamb.

*Garbolos.* Ah, who comes here?

*Comos.* There is much mixture in this tribe. Halt, who are ye ?

Paulos, Hush! Ye cannot tell but they maybe a Roman in disguise!

*Garbolos.* Hush thy fears, Paulos. [Enter Crimmerii and tribe.]

*Comos.* By heaven, there is much freedom in this fellow's gait.

*Paulos.* Let them pass.

*Comos.* This is no weed of earth that springs its seed from the rude gale of circumstances, or fastens life on chance.

*Garbolos.* Speak to them, Coinos, as they approach.

*Paulos.* No, let them pass on; they are not of our people! Let them go!

*Comos.* Halt! Strangers, where will ye ? Whom doth ye represent ?

*Crimmerii.* We? we represent a tribe of men, filling an engagement

*Comos.* Whom—what tribe are ye?

*Crimmerii.* A distant set, that prowl this country o'er in search of all that's beautiful. We let not the little primrose pass without a recognition; for we are told we are so benighted in our laws, that goodness cannot grow, or knowledge live, where we set foot, or honor thrive, when the rude hand of daily toil besmears it o'er with labor! Ha, ha! Braggart, wilt thou question me? They call us, Barbarians !

*Garbolos.* Who art thou. man—who art thou?

Crimmerii. Me ?

*Comos.* Yes—what name do ye go by?

*Paulos.* Chiefs, I tell thee let this man go; there is no good in all this question-ing. O, ye fareboding moon !

Crimmerii Name! I have no name by which the world docs know me yet. In fact, I have no name worth telling of.

*Garbolos.* Art thou with Icenia. decided?

*Crimmerii.* Who ?

*Comos.* Boadicia !

*Crimmerii.* Boadicia, Queen of Icenia ?

*Comos.* Yes.

*Paulos.* I told ye these men were strangers. What next will come ? (Aside.)

*Crimmerii.* I am Boadicia's hope—her life !

Garbolos and Paulos. How!

*Comos.* Speak out, man!

*Crimmerii.* I am her people; on them she well depends; her will prompts my deeds and sanctions them!

*Comos.* I see—a noble thought!

*Garbolos.* Then we act as friends !

*Crimmerii.* No—I am her friend; to you I am a stranger. Men, are ye done with me ?

*Garbolos.* Yes.

*Crimmerii.* Then am I free to pass ?

*Comos.* Yes; pass on.

*Paulos.* He is insulting. Are we not known to every clan as Chiefs?

*Crimmerii.* A want of thought, good Chiefs, or I might say, a want of knowledge of each other's spheres, might be rovoking to our dignities; but since the poor mind is weak to all the fears of etiquette, and titled foolery ! we might with pleasure oft construe offences into blessings and make neglect, with its regrets more pleasing to us all. [Exit.]

*Comos.* Now, who is this man ?

*Paulos.* A brute; I am insulted !

*Garbolos.* A god, in otter hid !

*Comos.* There rests in that man's heart more thought than fills up twenty such loose vain things as ye, Paulos. Art thou insulted? Aye, I'll hold a secret watch upon his inarch, and see wherewith the fates do lead him; for I have much opinion of his assistance to the Queen ! And see— his path leads to the plains of Bumairs, where we with promise held, were to meet the Queen at midnight. I'll follow him, and see if in his mind he has not held this same engagement. For methinks there is more in this man than we have seen.

*Garbolos.* And I'll with thee, Comos.

*Paulos.* I'll not be left alone, but will with thee for sake of company.

*Comos.* Oh, forgive me, Paulos; I should have asked thee through respect, I suppose, to keep with us thine engagement with the Queen. So come along, Paulos; ha, ha, ha !

*Garbolos.* Ha, ha ! The moon and compliment, Paulos !

*Paulos.* Tease me not with my defects. Advance, if you would have me follow.    [Exit all.]

ACT 1.

SCENE II.—A beautiful Garden near the Queen's residence— All in rustic beauty, but in the style of the times.

***Enter Pernios, Garbolos and Camperi.***

*Camperi.* Where left ye our friend Comos?

*Garbolos.* 'Neath yonder grove, where the brown shade and a sweet tongue lay wait upon his march, to check his heart a while.

*Camperi.* And he was from your company drawn by the fair face of a wayside wench ! Who whispers weakness in his cars ?

*Garbolos.* She was a creature fair to look upon, but having courteous Paulos with me as a friend, I was compelled to keep the bidden path, and walk herewith regretingly.

*Camperi.* Then, ha, ha ! Paulos, we must thank thee for these fine-timed notices of the man.

*Paulos.* No!

*Camperi.* "What? No!

*Paulos.* Yes !

*Camperi.* "Well, I thought I should be yes, for I have known this rogue, Garbolos, methinks, in other tricks than this.

*Paulos.* I mean no.

*Camperi.* No !

*Paulos.* Yes ! No !

*Camperi.* Ha, ha! yes ! no! and no! yes! Pah! (Claps Paulos familiarly on the shoulder.)

*Paulos.* Hold, familiar man !

*Camperi.* How ? Show some benevolence.

*Paulos.* I cannot laugh to-day.

*Camperi.* Why. Garbolis. what is this ?

*Garbolos.* He's seen something; the moon I think, or some other curious thing; his star's not bright to-day.

*Camperi.* Come, Paulos. tell us what's all this about ?

*Paulos.* Fear's shadow hangs o'er me. No light can brighten up my soul! No pride can stimulate its principle; for my spirit sinks into recipes of conceit, and sanctifies prediction in fear and sorrow !

*Camperi.* Tush, Paulos; some evil agency of Pluto beckons thee.

*Paulos.* I am as proof 'gainst Pluto as thou; man, mock me not!

*Camperi.* Great Jove ! There was more glory in that rebut than one could see by holding thee for hours in easiness. Ah, but see; here comes good Comos.

*Garbolos.* Aye, in company.

*Camperi.* Aye, let's us aside, nor overhear this secret caucusing. It's not our care.  [All exit.]

*Enter Comos and Alanthus.*

*Alanthus.* Then, Comos, must we part forever? Forever, Comos !

*Comos.* I hope not, Alanthus, and yet perchance it maybe forever.

*Alanthus.* I fear so, Comos.

*Comos.* Ye fear so ! Why ?

*Alanthus.* You know 'tis nature in our race to breed and brood up many thoughts, unkindred like to truth, and strangers far from reason and from the fancies of weak mind, will give them decided life.

*Comos.* But, Alanthus, thou art not such, daughter of Crimmerii.

*Alanthus.* No: so you have told me oft. Yet. Comos, I in my dream, which but a night ago, saw thee in blood, a maniac.

*Comos.* What, in desperate fig-lit. full of glory's thought, and thee, Alauthus ?

*Alanthus.* No, Comos. but on the earth in stiffened death, lay all that I call honored, Comos; and no friend was near; all deserted, except the loose lain samples of once brave madmen, unfortunate like thee, ambitious for death.

*Comos.* Banish such dreams; they are but dreams! dreams, the most flimsey facts of a weakened brain.

*Alanthus.* How; me, Comos?

*Comos.* Sweet Alanthus, banish all such thought! I pray thee banish dreams, the myths that would these fears arouse, for satisfaction would choke thee with them for thy belief, for the same ends; then laugh at thee.

*Alanthus.* Then, Comos, go and be a noble Chief. Fight the battles of the brave; be great, be proud, be what the world would have thee be—be honored ! And I will, with the meekness of the dove live on in bitter ease, and nurse the fears my mind hath caught, till ye return again. Go, Comos, to the war !

*Comos.* And wilt thou be happy in thy quiet cot, while I am jostled in the ranks of war?

*Alanthus.* Happy! yes. happy as the lone tigress that mourns its loneliness, and dreams over the strange fate of its stolen mate, which some idle hand hath caught to form the pastime of an hour, to please a loud laughing set that circles them around on every side, in merry ecstacies. Go, Comos. Go—yes, I will be happy! ah, happy!

*Comos.* Would that I had not this promise given unto the Queen; then would I saved ye this distress. [Kisses.]

*Alanthus.* Go, Comos; hast thou not promised such? Let me not see ye falter in this your promise; else little hope will I contain that ye'll return again, Co, Comos, go; and if thou art spared, come to me again as ye have promised. I will evade the snares of time which shall us separate, and greet thee pleasantly on thy return. Go, Comos, go !

*Comos.* Thanks, thanks, sweet Alanthus; thou hast nerved me doubly strong by thy encouragement. To battle will I go, with this economy of thought: "Spare all to whom life is dear!" that they may spare me for Alanthus' sake! for thee, Alanthus !

*Alanthus.* Noble Comos ! be foremost in the van; let not one hair fall back in cowardice! and gaze upon thy foe with that quiet look of the cooing dove, from out those eyes o'er which the lien cowers.

*Comos.* Then must we part; the hour is past and I must hasten onward.

*Alanthus.* Farewell! [Embrace]

*Comos.* Farewell; alas, farewell! [Comos retreats slow and silently.]

*Alanthus.* Farewell, Comos ! now he has gone forever! Never will he return ! Ah, ye powers of the fates of men, why do ye grow them through this life to such fair shapes, then hew them down like drunken things, with the dread blade of death? Oh! [weeps.] All beauty fades at night; so fades all hope when death is evident. The rose, the leaf, the pride, the glory, the manhood, the day, the sun, the stars, aye, and earth itself, seem but to float for a little while; then, disappear forever ! So must we all have our little day, then crumble with the dust of earth and be as common clay again ! Aye, as fates of all prove this a fact, I will no longer dream on its realities, but hie me to my little cot, and wait—and wait—and wait—ah, I would say, wait till he returns again ! No, no, no ! He will not return !

I'll follow him ! Yes, I'll follow him !   [Exit.]

Enter Boadicia—it grows dark—her Daughters are with her.

*Boadicia.* Thus turn we steps toward decision, and clear a pathway for the great that posterity shall bring; within whose eyes will glory rest; within whose heart shall protection grow, to shield the faults of woman—and for her weakness—which is too much love—load her with jewelled honors and attention

*Incia.* Mother, it is growing dark; sec how big the trees are.

*Boadicia.* Children, have no fear.

Lacia. Mother, I hear a noise; mother—

*Boadicia.* Be quiet, children; complain not yet, for we have many days ahead well clothed in doubts and fears, and noisy revelry!

*Incia.* Mother, there is men; see them?

*Boadicia.* Where, child ?

*Incia.* Do you not see them ? Yonder from the wood they come.

*Boadicia.* Yes, I see them now; they are friends; be not alarmed. How quick the timid eye of youth hears to a feeble heart. O God, protect and give to my liege some holy confidence, that they, in this sad hour of trial, may brave hell's every action, and live at peace with God—should live resigned to every circumstance—provoking, in their quiet mien, fear's every effort!

**Enter Paulos. Garbolos and Camperii.**

Ah !—Now must I meet these friends with much sober feeling, and soften them to the good will of honest Charity ! Welcome, Chiefs; proud nobles of a fearful race, advance !

Paulos [Kneels.] Most gracious Queen, Paulos, Chief of Brigantes, joins thee !

Garbolos [Kneels.] Most favored Queen, Garbolos. Chief of Congi, joins thee !

Camperi [Kneels.] Most noble Queen, Camperi, Chief of Silerus, joins thee !

*Boadicia.* Chiefs, with blessings on ye, arise ! Why loosen ye thy courteous knee in such deep compliment ? Is it necessary ?

*Garbolos.* We follow Paulos in politeness.

*Camperi.* Yea, he is more used to its weak forms than we.

*Paulos.* The heart should show to every man, his duty to a woman.

*Boadicia.* Chiefs, avoid this ceremony; it imitates too much the mockery of state and Roman bondage. We are a people born to bear the point and butt of coming good. Show reverence, but mock not yourselves, my noble men, by the vile imitation of the base, who court and prop the coffers of the great, for sake of sacrifice. No ! Be men ! Be Chiefs ! Be what the gods would have thee be—be men ! Men ! know ye that word ? It holds more honor in this world, 'mid these wicked times, than all the gilded givings of the great, so harnessed up in tinsel. Yes; be men; not fawning, crouching dogs, who would lick the public feet for plunder ! No, Chiefs, I hope ye are not such; for if ye are, ye are not the men I sent for, or have I any counsel with ye ! Go home !

*Camperi.* Then have we dropped the plummet to its depth.

Paulas. Most gracious Queen, forgive all our offences.

*Boadicia.* With that charity of soul which woman hath, I forgive ye all; yet ye offend me not.

*Garbolos.* Most gracious Queen, we did use this craft of ceremony to fathom out the mind whereon we were to lean. Had we partook of the rough customs of our native suit, we could not thus have told how far the devil with our prospects ran.

*Boadicia.* Most wise and cunning Chiefs; like serpents wouldst thou wisdom hide, 'neath the soft feathers of the gentle dove But be wise, to all things, for much wisdom will we need, and much gentleness. Is it not known among the clans, that the foul hands of Home hath dealt severely with us; aye, from the dead howl of dark complaints that fill my ear, from morn till night; that there is sorry times in Britton's Isle ? Gentlemen, is there no physic at hand— no redress ?

All. Yes—yes !

*Boadicia.* Aye, the wild flame of fear and hate doth madly rush 'cross hill and dale, when but two moons ago we pastured with that sweet content that only summer minds can know, that bloom with peace and plenty. Chiefs, justice and the laws of man demand a sacrifice. Let it be what it will, I am prepared !

*Garbolos.* And I!

*Camperi.* And I!

*Paulos.* And I!

*Boadicia.* Then let this be resolved, that honest minds, pure, honest deeds, and walks upright withal, not fearing to step aside for truth.

*All.* Hail, glorious Queen; thy people all in thee here chosen !

*Camp.* In thee have we centered all, ere this interview could lend its aid to prove our wisdom in it.

*Garb.* Aye, thy people all, from East, from West, from North, from South, doth boldly side with thee, and ask for thy protection.

*Boad.* Whyfore ask they all of me ? Me, a woman ! a widowed Queen !

*Garb.* In thee will they every hope confide; in battle follow only thee.

*Boad.* Me, the leader of a war, in battle charging unto death? War! war! Ah! what horrors hath that name e'er sent into my soul, e'er since my tongue did first learn its true interpretation.

*Garb.* Thus have they all decided.

*Incia.* See, mother, people running this way.

*Lucia.* Mother, what does this mean ?

*Boad.* Be quiet, children; fear not. Oh, that I could keep thee in ignorance of thy fate ! Be calm, I will protect thee.

**Enter a band of Barbarians, in confusion and fear.**

*Camp.* Hold ! Why this intrusion ?

*Boad.* Good people, why this haste ? Is there good news, that ye do come with such eager steps ?

*Barb.* Good news ! Fire, murder, treason, stealing, lying, cheating! Oh! good news? Look we like good news? Don't mock us, woman; don't mock us, I say !

*Boad.* I hope I do not bar from thee that good will which I would thee show, and see, in every act of mine toward my countrymen, Mock thee ! No. Pity thee! No; for that is hypocrisy and pride. But, I charge thee, why art thou here ? Answer,

*Barb.* For thee; for thee, Boadicia, our Queen !

*All the Tribe.* For thee—for thee!

*Barb.* Lead us to revenge, and food, or see us die like dogs, performing the demands of cruel necessity, who sports in our misfortune, and name us brutes for our good faithfulness.

*Boad.* I understand. Retire. There's a motive which shall test all the true sects of Rome. Meet me at midnight by the half gromecirclc, along the Meni, where we will this night resolve, whether it be best to tamper with our ills, 'neath virtue's scowl, and cheat this coming hope [to [to her children,] of its free choice and merry day:—or battle with the darkening cloud that hangs o'er heath and home, and drive it as the morning sun drives back the thickening clouds of night, which opens to our fair view the sky, the earth, the world, in all its living glorious hues, when the sweet carol of the morning bird, the sweet perfume of the fragrant rose, make up these mornings of our lives, in consummated joy.

*All.* To battle ! To battle !

*Boad.* Then meet me at midnight, beside the Meni. Away !

*All.* Hail, Boadicia! Queen Boadicia !   [Exit.

*Boad.* Now, Chiefs, as I have this band dispersed, to form again beside the Meni, let me so direct ye, that we may in our council meet, and in our faith decide.

*Camp.* May faith with good success decide, and name thee conqueror, Queen of all.

*Garb.* There shall be no drawback to success: For honor thrives when most contended, And shame shrinks most when best defended.

*Paulos.* Aye, may the gods devote us to success. Farewell.

*Garb.* Farewell.

*Camp.* Farewell.        [Exit all.

*Boad.* Farewell, till midnight. Now must I this little time improve, and balance in this little space my life's in tentions; for the word is spoken, and every clan and every tongue speaks loudly forth for war. War! How many hearts must bleed at this decision ! How many new-made graves will Britain hold! Aye, it needs some thought to reckon up this sacrifice. But good it is; distress oft walks in pity's clothes, amidst the fairest fields, and poisons with its venomed breath sweet incense in the bud, and stops the bloom of loveliness from fodder for the worms ! So comes troubles for us all! Unseen, they come; unseen, they go ! So come and go all life! So came we; so goeth we! Come, children, to thy home. [Exit]

**Enter Alanthus from the Wood.**

*Alanthus.* Then this was Boadicia; she, for whom my Comos fights, to whom I sacrifice my only joy. I"ll follow in her path and scent the spot where Comos is, and see him again before he dies! Poor Comos, my father did thee much offend; but thou art brave, and I will recompense all his misdoings. And these Chiefs—all, all for Boadicia die! What a magnificent offering! No! Where is my father's arm? Father! far in old Anglesea ! King of her renown! Comos, but thy slave! Thy daughter's life!— Comos. I'll fly to thee!

**End of Scene 2.**

## ACT 1

SCENE III.—Along the banks of the Meni Straits, within a Druid Circle, half dilapidated—Crimmerii and his Chiefs discovered in much good feeling—Moon just rising—Time midnight— Torches burning.

*Crimmerii.* [Enter 1st Chief] Saw you no signs of their approach ? 'Tis midnight.

*1st Chief* Methinks I saw on yonder hill, some figures bending hard this way, and looking back at the full moon, to calculate as one would think, the distance they had gained upon the lion's side. (Chiefs all laugh.)

*Crim.* They should have choosed a slower steed than the bright moon, for it has distanced them already, and sit with us. I fear they're tardy in the limb, and limp for conscience sake, which may well keep them from decision and committal. They're understanding dogs! (Chiefs laugh.) *For conscience oft weakens every nerve, while honor would keep the mind most desperate. Tut, for such braggarts ! Aye, and Comos, he would have like a lion roared, had we bid well to tarry. You'll yet see him like a bleating calf.* (All laugh.)

*Enter Comos.*

*Comos.* Why this loud laughter? One would well think that from the uproar of your noisy throats, which stint the evening air with its putrid breath, ye had much ill-bred feasting 'mong ye, instead a council for the world! Are ye upon a spree ? Speak; who are ye ?

*Crim.* A merry one, ah!

*Comos.* This was the boor we stopped upon the moor. Man, what was all this noise about ?

*Crim.* That which did catch thine ear as thou wert passing ?

*Comos.* Yea, as I approached.

*Crim.* Nothing worth telling ye.

*Comos.* Not civil; I came by an appointment of Queen Boadicia, to meet in solemn confidence.

*Crim.* And I.

*Comos.* You ?

*Crim.* Aye, and all this band.

**Enter Paulos, Garbolos and Camperi.**

*Garb.* Comos, thou hast beaten us in this rough march, and deserve the honor for thy first arrival.

*Comos.* No, this man was here ahead of me. I aimed to be the first.

*Camp.* Who?

*Comos.* He whom we met at the break of morn upon the moor.

*Camp.* Ah !

*Garb.* Hast thou found of whom he is ?

*Comos.* No.

*Paulos.* Handle this man with care, for methinks he is of dangerous stuff.

*Comos.* Pooh, Paulos, pooh.

*Paulos.* But handle him with gloves, good Comos.

*Garb.* Hush, Paulos; thou wouldst breed more devils in men's ears than spiders in twenty hatchings.

*Crim.* (aside.) Then these are my associates ! Ah, here comes the Queen.

Comos, &c. The Queen—the Queen arrives !

***Enter Boadicia and several Monks and Priests of the Druids.***

*Crim.* Let her hold and have all reverence.

*Paulos.* My heart be with it.

*Comos.* And mine.

*Camp.* And mine.

*Garb.* And mine.

Boadicia adcances toward the Chief Priest—the Chiefs all hail, except Crimerii, &c.

*Crim.* Bray on. ye asses.

*Boad.* Be quiet. Chiefs. Loud clamor ill becomes so serious an event. If in ye rests the silence of good minds, keep ye on that side for wisdom's sake; and think ye often ere ye loose your breath in base affright, to scare the stooping bat, or force the gentle sleeping bird from its warm nest, to let cold creeping terror in to nurse them to decay! (Approaches the High Priest and kneels.) Most Holy Father! teach me in the growth of thought, and pencil on my mind the figures of destiny—of decision, of charity—that I may gain protection for my heritage, and clothe them in that free hope which is as dear to me and them as the soft beatings of the inner life.

*Priest.* Queen of Ieenia—there is a power above us all which blessed thee in thy birth, by making thee an inheritant to sorrow Push not aside from the afflictions of mankind; these arc but temporary, which cling to all, and expose to sight much wisdom, developed in this little will we live in. But there is a power divine, more holy still than all, that shapes us unto every fault and every favor, and rules us with a common good, with justice to emergency. Arise, (arises) go ye in prosperity! consummate thy people's hopes ! redeem thy name—thy honor—and poets will parise thee in songs of fame, and make thee in grace descend to the fair days where honor shines in glory's crown ! Go ye hence in faith, hope and charity, in blessings and in prosperity!

*Boad.* Thanks, most holy lather.

*Priest.* Go, thy people wait for thee.

*Boad.* Chiefs, advance! The hour has come when we must strike for Britain and Equality! Home and Nationity! Peace and Posterity ! Came ye here for this ? (Alanthus is seen stealing and secreting herself behind a tree.) ***Came ye here to judge of superiority and right ? Let them who do decide with nature's laws prove their responsibility. We must not lag in this decision; time flies on wings of light, and soon will usher in the smiling face of morn, and turn our midnight's conference to the eyes of open day. We must be brief and finish up this work, or else be caught in our own net, for want of energy, else there's no proof in proverbs ! Chiefs, why met ye here, and made to figure in this scene ? Speak as thou art prompted.*** (Pause.)

*Alanthus.* (aside.) Why does not Comos speak?

*Paulos.* (advances.) ***Most gracious Queen: a common evil have we all im-***

*bibed, which, from its work upon us all, of which we all complain, seems firmly held into our sight by the mailed herd of Rome, who, but twenty moon's ago, we looked upon as a protector, who proves more heinous in his good, than Pluto in the eyes of death ! I speak for all Brigantes.* (Retires.)

*Alanthus.* (aside.) Now, Comos next. No !

Garb. (advances.) *Most gracious Queen: I came as brother, sent with friend Paulos, to speak into your ear my people's sufferings, that ye may form, from out their sadness and distress, some stuff or substance of partition, wherewith ye may from Nero claim some compensation for the misdeeds of his foul slaves, who lord us with impunity, I speak for all Coegi.* (Retires.)

*Alanthus.* How, no Comos yet? (Aside.)

*Camp.* Most gracious Queen: I do submit to the plain sight of simple reasoning, the miseries of our race, which from the facts recorded, reach high into the eyes of shame, and choke the mouth of pity. By its rank perfidy, which grows in dark luxuriance, and spreads its poisoned breath o'er old Silenus, giving death at every breath, with silent poison. I speak to you of all Silenus, whom I offer and represent. (Retires.)

*Alanthus.* Ah, Comos ! ah, he conies ! Be still, glad heart! Comos ! (Comos advances.)

*Comos.* Good and gracious Queen: I offer you the right of all Langolon, of whom I represent. They are at your disposal! Use them and me at thy discretion ! (Retires.)

*Alanthus.* What! has Comos no more to say? So brief! so eloquent!

*Boad.* (a silence.) *And is there no more among ye ?* [Crimmerii is seen talking with his Chiefs.] No more that gives to justice hope ? Have ye all spoken I Chiefs, are ye done !

*Crim.* (advances.) No! [Much sensation of indignation among Comos, $ c.]

*Alanthus.* (aside.) His voice—hark !

Road. Stranger ! If thou, too, art in bondage and would be free, speak, and we will give thee freedom and rest!

*Crim.* How?

*Alanthus.* O, heavens, I fear !

Road. By the strong arm of justice, which, nerved by the free will of a thinking populace, will snap asunder the despotic links of shame, infamy, poverty and distress, which chains us all to earth.

*Crim.* Woman! [Sensation with Comos, &.c.]

*Comos.* Chiefs, this is insulting!

*Boad.* Chiefs should show much charity!

*Crim.* Men, spare thy anger and contentions.

*Boad.* Stranger, if thou hast aught to speak, proceed; for thy delay but riles good courtesy.

*Crim.* Most august Queen, of good Prestages: I come at thy invitation, with friends to suffer with and conceal thy every artifice in war.

*Alanthus.* O, ye gods, protect my Comos ! Aye, 'tis he!

*Crim.* We come from distant homes to share thy every grief.

*Alanthus.* Father?

*Crim.* Hark, that voice! it was familiar. Heard you not a voice ?

*Boad.* It was but the passing wind.

*Crim.* We seek no popularity in this contest, or stoop to the low decencies of life for thanks. We offer with the will of men, not with the pride of titled Chiefs, for they are trash! trash! who offer to fight with thee, a woman ! We came to fight for thee, and give thee the victory ! We ask no compensation for allegiance to a just cause, in breaking down the yoke of tyranny! We came not with woman's hearts, but time-honored Chiefs, who sport the blood of great Caroctus ! And, from his last advice, " Help ye one another," came here to join thy standard, add thy cause to justify!

*Boad.* Thanks, brave Chief.

*Comos.* Who is this in secretion! Who treats us with such mean civility?

*Crim.* Me !

*Alanthus.* O, Comos, hold ! Would that I could touch thee.

*Comos.* Aye, if thou art no spy, expose thyself, or by the laws of our creation I do demand redress ! [About to draw, also Paulos, Ca?npcri and Garbolos.]

*Crim.* Ha, ha, ha ! Put up thy weapon, boy. Shame ! Fools ! See you not I am not single-handed? Shame upon ye ! Use thought, rash youth !

*Garb.* I do, from the wise Queen, entreat an explanation.

*Boad.* Chiefs!

*Crim.* Silence, I command!

*Comos.* By heavens, none shall command but Boadicia!

*Crim.* Down, slave! I am thy King! [Disguise falls off.]

*Boad.* Hail, Crimmeri, King of Anglesea ! [His Chiefs all hail.]

*Alanthus.* (rushing out.) ***O, father, spare good Comos J*** [Comos, &c., have kneeled at the feet of Crimmerii]

*Crim.* What, my child, art thou here!

*Comos.* Alanthus! (Rises.)

*Alanthus.* O, forgive him, father, I pray thee forgive him ! forgive good Comos, for thy daughter's sake, forgive him.

*Crim.* I forgive him. (She kisses.) ***For thy mother's image, I forgive thee and give thy request.*** (Her father then embraces with Comos.) Go, and from this hour learn much wisdom dwells in homeliness; that greatness, with its talent, knows the value of its underclothes, and minds well stored by honest toil, will not from borrowed wits recoil, so soon as pride unfounded Go ye in peace.

*Paulos.* Great King, your pardon.

*Camp.* We seek your pardon.

*Garb.* Pardon, King.

*Crim.* Arise! We pardon for offences! ye have none yet committed. But I—I seek your pardon for offences. (Kneels.)

*All.* Hail, Crimmerii, King of Anglesca ! Hail, Boadicia, Queen of Icenia! Long live the King! Long live the Queen!

*Crim.* Alanthus, Queen Boadicia.

*Boad.* Welcome, daughter of a noble sire, proud offspring of a noble race— meet Cherubim of god's !

*Crim.* Chiefs ! [All his Chiefs advance, disguise off, and form on his right—C. and C form on his left, with Boadicia, Priests and Alanthus—his soldiers unfurl the banner of Carotins.]

Boad, Hail, ye emblem of freedom—hail, sacred relic of Caroctus !

*All.* Hail, hail, hail!

*Crim.* Silence! If I command, let me here say, now is the hour drawing near when we must retire, else caught we be for want of goodly action. Let the Queen relate her proposition, and beneath this banner of Liberty, let each district pledge its firm support to uphold its Union—one and inseparable !

*All.* The Queen—the Queen ! (Alanthus joins Comos.)

*Boad.* Then to this conclusion have I drawn my every reasoning, that Britain suffers crimes unjust from an intruding hand, who claims but hospitality, yet un-scrupulously doth rob our very sustenance; enslaves our race, imprisons our chiefs, disregards our laws, and treats us all contempt, ously, and think us but a brutish set, set lower by our meekness. I have resolved that, by the second moon, I will to London go, and claim from great Prustanus some appeal, some privilege of his oath, some portion of his promise, some part of Nero's favor, long promised to Icenia's King, my dead Prestagus. What say you, Chiefs, to this !

*Garb.* Make the time sooner, while courage is in battle heat, for fear of a reaction, which delay oft betrays.

*Boad.* Then, when shall it be ?

*Grim.* On tomorrow's morn.

*Boad.* So soon ?

*Crim.* Sooner the better.

*Boad.* And my children ?

*Crim.* They shall with thee, for innocence touches the hard heart more sharp with its supplications than spears of glittering steel.

*Boad.* Then be it so. Alone, I haste with the speed of thought, and free my people's miseries, if there be pity in this man's soul. If not, I'll to my home retire, and saddle up for war ! War! O, horrid war !

*Crim.* No, not alone. I'll send thee guarded, though thou alone shall have no fear from the pranks of Senatus. Remember—tomorrow, at break of day, depart for London. Tomorrow—the sun shall rise and brighten that proud thought —speed thee on thy journey, to battle with all fearful Rome, and Roman prejudices ! O, Rome! how beautiful methinks the day will be, when Rome is resting in her solemn grave ! (Alanthus steals to her father's side, while he is repeating this soliloquy.)

When bright Aurora comes prancing forth upon her chariot of fire, and drives her fleeting steeds with lightning flash through the blue vaults of day! And as she dips her glowing wheel behind the western wave, methinks she gives new light to nations yet unheard to man ! who'll give impetus to the world with greater speed than time ! and raise the standard of the man above his common theme! and make in him all enterprise, civilization, liberty and trust!

*Alanthus.* Father, will this be in my day ?

*Crim.* No, my child. 'Tis nations yet unborn, who sleep yet in their mother's womb—unnamed, unknown—save to the gods of destiny! (Day begins to break.)

*Boad.* Chiefs: the morning lights up yonder east with certainty. Seek thy resorts, and wait with patient thoughts and sober hours on the decrees of Rome.

(Allbid farewell around— Comos and Alanthusjoin—Crimmerit and Boadicia join—the other Chiefs return each other's recognition.) This council is at end.

*Alanthus and Comos walk off*—Boadicia and Priests, Crimmerit and Chiefs, Garbolos, Camperi and Paulos—the Sun rises on the scene, as the curtain falls, revealing a beautiful landscape—Birds are singing—all seems beautiful, revealing the true stage of the Welch customs, and a corcect picture of wild Anglasian scenery.

*Crim.* The day cometh when we must separate. Let each his occupation seek, giving much good report from sober industry and predestined will. Chiefs, follow me.

Let conscience govern virtue's part,

And wisdom fill each generous heart,

The love which guides the soul of man

Will honor and protect thee—woman.          [Exit.]

***Enter two Priests.***

*1st Priest.* Too many oaths already sworn, too many lies already told, makes truth with falsehood say, amen.

*2nd Priest.* But if we swear by it ?

*1st Priest.* Fain would I swear by every oath that's holy, if such an act could avail the consummation of our purpose.

*2d Priest.* Will not prayers with the law avail ?

*1st Priest.* The law—the law ! Why, how long have you lived ? Fudge for the law ! More devils hide within the codes, with safe conceit and golden favor, than justice ever dreamed of. Good men and the laws are kin, but ruffians seize its legacies and profession.

*2d Priest.* Ah, no; not so cruel, good Pious.

*1st Priest.* Rip up the fringe which fashion wears in a profession so divine, and ye will find it threadbare worn, from the soft feet of mean hypocrisy.

*2d Priest.* But we should not the warp expose, to prove the face the fabric wears.

*1st Priest.* No, but we should contrast, then compare, and show the profit with the price, and see if quality gives prudence leave to speculate and own,

*2d Priest.* Why, ha, ha, ha! You would a monger here assume, and traffic for your rights in law as produce in the mart.

*1st Priest.* All things are bought and sold. The public mind with public power propose a price twice figured.

*2d Priest.* Ha, ha, ha! and ye would cheat a little with it all, I fear, good Pious.

*1st Priest.* Keep quiet, Dobbin; you've struck a truth at last; if we would our bacon save, must cheat with gravity.

*2d Priest.* And leave immediately.     [Exit.]

*End of Act I.*

# ACT II.

SCENE I.— A woody grove not far from London—London in the distance, with a distant view of the surrounding country — View of the River Thames, $.c.

*Enter Boadicia and her turo Daughters.*

*Boad.* Thus far have we succeeded well. [It gradually grows dark.] The city is in sight; a blessed loveliness ! Ah, that the day would but hold on till we had closed this little space, which ends our pilgrimage.

*Incia.* Mother, I am tired and sleepy.

*Boad.* Sweet child, thou shalt rest here for the night.

*Incia.* Oh, dear mother, do not leave us here.

Lacia. No, mother, no.

**_Boad._** Innocence, what shouldst thou fear ? We cannot reach the city, and the broad gates will be closed upon us; none arc allowed to enter after the sun goes down. 'Tis safer in this quiet place than by the busy walls of yonder troubled city, for danger lurks where power sleeps. So I will hide thee here, and gather fresh herbs for thy repast. Be of good cheer; I'll soon return. [Exit Boadicia—children lean upon the ground and fall asleep.]

**_Enter Crimmerii, disguised as a Roman._**

**_Crim._** How, abandoned ! No, there is too much assurance in this sleep; she must be somewhere here about. Ah, no. Methought I heard her step ! Sleep on, innocence! Oh, how happy is the sight of this. Here rests two kingdoms in one grasp. How oft a jewel lies within our reach, yet we well fatted to the ignorant customs of this life, know not when opportunity affords such offerings in infant greatness. Sleep on, sweet infancy ! Did but the tyrant of yon hell know that thou wert lying so near his door in all thy purity, how would he act? Oh, Paulaius, the world may thank thee for a conscience friendly with sleep, that blinds thy soul for a little while from the dark crafts of wickedness; else little would I give for Boadicia's hope. Ah, she comes. Now must I every artifice employ, and test her resolution.

**_Enter Boadicia._**

Now, impudence, thy power claim, And test the strength of woman's aim. (Assumes the fool.)

I care not for the Ce-ze-ze-zar,

No, not a bit care I.

Or does the Ce-ze-ze-zar

Care one d——d bit for I.

Ah, woman—ha-ha—woman.

*Boad.* Stranger, hold; thy conduct speaks thee not proper sane. What art thou ? Art thou a Roman ?

*Crim.* Ah, good lady, ha-ha-ha; quite glad to meet you, ha-ha-ha; what news have ye from London? He-he, the hour runs late

*Boad* Keep thy distance, man. (Aside.) Am I the doubts of duping men ? If thou art from the city, speak; what news is there in London ?

*Crim.* London did you say, or St. Albans ? Boad. I did say Landon; what more? (Aside.) I have suspicions of this man.

*Crim.* Why, how funny. London, hey, London, London. Bowl. Man, tamper not with me. I am no silly wanderer in midnight's trail. If thou have aught to speak, speak it plainly—manly Crim. Ah; ha-ha! Boad. I hold no fear from shame.

*Crim.* Ah; ha-ha!

*Boad.* Thou imitatest that low born set that feed the stomach 'till it pains, ne'er dreaming of that little thought that builds the soul of man, but feast and drudge in wayside ills, like brutes in common, dreaming; then sleep and serve their time away, and grow fat withal. Pass on.

*Crim.* Good woman, have pity, have pity on a fool! He, though he be cursed with seeming fate by doing what his nature leads him—have pity; a little pity! What is it? It is—it is, the soul of woman ! If thou hast a soul within thee, and love it, blaspheme me not! No, no; for I am equally in the god's care as thou, and as well cared for.

*Boad.* This is a curious mixture. Wert thou born a man. a Roman ?

*Crim.* A child—ha-ha; a        . No, I'll tell no more; ha-ha. Actions speak thy fear, but have no fear on my account; I'll not tell of thee; no, I'll keep closed house on news. Go on with thy purpose; ye'll find mo proof, though I were a Roman. Ha-ha; proceed.

*Boad.* What means all this ?

*Crim.* Woman, when wilt thou be what nature has decreed thee—ah ?

*Boad.* now?

*Crim.* Ah, I fear never; no, no !

*Boad.* What is this ye preach ? If there be aught to reason with, tell it, tell it plainly, meaningly. Pain me not thus.

*Crim.* Woman, send a keener eye into the moving, thinking' world, and mark its destiny; see woman as she is and as she should be! Look to thyself; be what thou wert when given to partake of the good life; be what thou shouldst be—no more; and act thy part more wisely, for the good of human kind.

*Boad.* What knowest thou of me?

*Crim.* Of thy shape, I see thee; of what thou art, the gods alone can tell. I know not thy mind; 'tis not my care; be honest to thyself, there is no fear. Thy name and all that is made up on earth to condemn thee, is with thee! What more, I know not; but have no fear; I'll not tell of thee; no, not I.

*Boad.* Stay, stranger; what is there in thy preachings ? Teach me.

*Crim.* Time will teach us; experience will criticise.

*Boad.* But I am a stranger to thy theory; no unbelief persuades me; I am in ignorance. If thou seest differently into myself from what I myself can see, explain, not conjecture.

*Crim.* Woman, O woman, marry good intent, and so fill woman's destiny. With prattling nature perched upon thy knee, to lisp thy joys and sorrows o'er in childish accent, and link more closely by thy marriage bands, thy immortal nature. Tune thy linnet voice with the golden harp, to sing the blessings of nuptial joys, at Cupid's kind request, for the good of woman.

*Boad.* All this have I done in sympathy complete, in purity and holy love.

*Crim.* Ah, be it so, well done!

*Boad.* Yea, a goodly portion; a two-fold treasure, in pleasure bound from golden infancy.

*Crim.* Ah!

*Boad.* Two delicious troubles—innocent and blessed !

Crim, Pardon, woman; if my words did hit thee, I meant them for thy good. So. if thou hast this noble institution of thyself built up, the fabric is complete. What more should woman wish, than be the mother of sweet babes, sweet home and calm repose ?

*Boad.* A shelter for her breeding; a warm and easy fold, to keep them from the breath of earth, that chills the finer thoughts of life, and binds us to the wheels of fate to sweat and toil in madness, that racks us with pain in every nerve; which binds us so low with the weight of shame, that occupation has no name and reputation no after-thought. (Weeps.)

*Crim.* (aside.) Ah, I see. Now have I her in much wretchedness ! If she has faith in her appeal, it will soon show itself, Is there nothing in thy acquaintances—hast thou got hope within thee?

*Boad.* Yes.

*Crim.* Art thou firm in thy affairs'?

*Boad.* Yes.

*Crim.* Think well before thou speakest; stand firm upon thy feet!

*Boad.* Pain me no more by questioning; I wish but to live.

*Crim.* What is this life to us unless we breed some good? Aye, and have a care withal, which keeps us friendly with obligation and respect.

*Boad.* Thy mystery distracts me !

*Crim.* Canst thou not think ? Hast thou not the soul of thought I Canst thou not cull the fairest points of reason ?

*Boad.* I understand not.

*Crim.* Go, shake the dust from off thy sandals into oppression's face, and ask as woman alone can ask, protection for thy heritage.

*Boad.* (aside) Much mystery clothes this man !

*Crim.* And if thou art refused, be prudent and go home.

Road. Home!

*Crim.* Aye, for such examples are worth more to this world, in all its wretched nakedness, than all the honored forms of mankind, clothed in black duplicity.

*Boad.* What duplicity is this ! This man is no fool!

*Crim.* Thy wanderings are magnificently mysterious ! thy pleadings methinks futile; thy purpose shall lead a world of thought to a glorious resurrection ! And man ! O man! what wilt thou be ? Perched on thy throne invincible ! inconceivable! intellectually sustained to spreading thy wings of mercy o'er sea and land sustaining divinity— wherein posterity shall rear her sons to noble contemplation; when soul shall execute the limits of the soul, by self-appreciation, and make the free-born limits of our kin a universal charge; that we may know unto ourselves the sweets of human liberties; when life shall be for life; and he that shields himself by death shall meet his own reward, and conscience reign our only king supreme, in universal suffrage !

*Boad.* Is this the conduct of Rome ? Roman, speak; thy boon seems but a burthen; is this 'mong Romans—all?

*Crim.* Romans are in every clime; their valor give them such. I talk to you in London; my soul rests in the little heaven of wild Anglesea !

*Boad.* How—ye ? Children of Rome, how be it—this thy conduct ? A wild notion that—thou hadst better stay at home. Look up—thy mother may thy absence mourn, and friends will wipe her swollen eyes from sorrow. I charge thee Roman rest not then till thou hast well decided.

*Crim.* I understand my part. We all get misled by time. It is no wonder a few should out of joint be led. The world holds fine allurements to the eager eye of man, and man by their like adopt, for sake of treatment than linger with the sickening of death and hellish Nero !

*Boad.* Hold, Roman, hold! the gods may see thee! 'Tis treason to blaspheme thy sovereign.

*Crim.* Hold, woman, hold to thy tongue! Turn from thy nature and consider. A little thought will cause thee wonder; a little time will show thee all; a little fear will cost thee nothing; to be too positive in haste, too sure, is dangerous. You are near by Romans; yet have no fear from me.

*Boad.* Presumptuous man, to whom wouldst thou dictate ? Think me but a feeble cringing woman? Am I one of your compulsory *things,* that give and listen to your lords of Rome, for beggared decency?

*Crim.* Woman!

*Boad.* Shame, on any shape that dared upbraid me ! Am I not of myself sustained ? The world bears hungry wonder on my track. Ye hounds of men bark fruitlessly. Is not woman capable of herself? Is she not what she should be? Ye lord it as in common man—as if no greater power taught thee.

*Crim.* Woman !

*Boad.* Why crawl ye into my path and hiss thy vague suspicions o'er into my face, and prick me with thy dastard cautions? Know I not the path of virtue? Shun I not the path of vice, which ye men's affections would drag me to, with little ceremony ? Go, go —wash thy hands of mockery —go!

*Crim.* Hear me, woman !

*Boad.* O thou bundle of "iniquity and rags," how dare ye stand within my presence, and here expose the triflings of thy guilty soul? Turn to thy duty, man. Be to thy country, its protector, and bathe thy tortuous wounds in blood of royal heroism. Let ye be of what descent ye may, turn to thy country's cause, be gone—away!

*Crim.* No, never. Though I were Roman born, and Roman like expressed, I would not side with Rome, as we express it. Though all the gods with Hector came, to blot the friendship of our cause, they would not in my mind sustain one moment's hesitancy; for wrought with flaws is every blessed coming, backed by impious laws, which bring us to our fill of shame. Let the earth in deathy whiteness bleach, let Ethiope her stains remove, they cannot, shall not teach me otherwise than love my country! But the base rulers which, for a day immortal, seem to hold diviner sway than common man, who spue their venom on the face of earth, and give a new hereditary birth to Rome's most valiant lineage !

*Boad.* Man, who art thou ?

*Crim.* Keep thy discretion closely drawn, nor cheat thy stern purpose with so bland a smile, and so deceive thy energy by too much confidence. This goodly helmet, this honored sword, is equal texture with my will and word ! Accept them all, me too include, and make me the base thing of servitude. My life I value all for thee ! Am I not a generous subject, Boadicia ?

*Boad.* How, and know me ! Who art thou ? From whence comes, thou ? What wouldst thou with me?

*Crim.* Advise, instruct, guard and protect.

*Boad.* Trove thy responsibility, then will I listen patiently and follow thy advice.

*Crim.* Hold to thy understanding; anxiety corrodes thy breast. Taint not thy milk with gross unkindness, for thy sucklings will vomit forth their firm dislike, scratch thee in the face, and call thee hateful, hateful mother!

*Boad.* How ?

*Crim.* Like we of Rome; from childhood grown to man, hate the fastidious rules of childhood, and like to be as men persuaded by our own judgments, and learn to recognize ourselves among men, manfully! The gag of Rome fits not the throat of freemen ! No, no.

*Boad.* What proof have I of thy individuality? (Crimmerits disguise drops.) The transformation is more of surprise than truth.

*Crim.* Wouldst thou know me by the name of Plusso? Boad. What. Plusso, and know me ? Ye gods protect me !

*Crim.* Woman, have no alarm, or it will move thee from the good thou hast intended Boad. Plusso! Plusso !

*Crim.* Hast thou heard of Plusso's name in other acts than good, that you so wondrously should stare at aught except the name? This shape ye saw an hour ago with less or no surprise; then why should you so crazy gaze ? Your glossy eyes look here in wonderment.

*Boad.* 'Twas with a question anxiety proposes: If here should friendship meet within these sober darkened cells, when aught but faith could creep, when confidence should stand in honor's noble clasp, and wipe away thy faults to man, in that familiar grasp of friendship ?

*Crim.* Not so fast, kind woman; thou art ever to be deceived by love and confidence. Friendship springs up like tender truant grass, which bends its green and willing blades toward the sunny side; it buds and blossoms; then full in bloom 'tis seen by every admiring eye; thro' beauty's sunny walks; soon the clouds assume a thickening change upon the bluish horizon; the winds waft gently by with nature's incense laden. Cloud piles on cloud; hark! there is a coming storm; heavy rolls the deafening thunders, crumbling, like a hundred earthquakes into one, convulsing heaven with earth and earth with heaven; the flaming darts like Etna flash high into the dome of ether blue, then back to earth with lightning driven, the angry bolt descends. Then all is still. The few first drops fall slowly, heavily; pat, pat, pat; like the first red drop that tells the gladiator's doom, a sickly quietness prevails. Friend looks at friend, then with a hurried glance shoot by, seek shelter from the coming storm; then trampling feet in haste doth crush the bloom of friendship in the dust, and leaves the mangled heath behind, seared by the scorch of a desert wind, to utter misery, to hope forlorn, all for friendship.

*Boad.* Plusso, give me advice; thy dictates shall prove my destiny.

*Crim.* Woman, thou art deceived ! Trust not the honey on the lip, for it may turn to bitterness in thy stomach. As I have cautioned thee remember, and be thou wise unto the morrow. Farewell.    [Exit.]

*Boad.* O stay, I pray thee; no, no; farewell, farewell. Now must I to my little brood return. (Enter Plusso.) *Oh, oh, oh.* (She weeps and retires.)

*Plusso discovers the children, who arise and meet him.*

*Incia.* Mother.

Plusso. I am not thy mother, child, or thy father. Where is thy mother ?

*Incia.* She left us there to sleep till she returned.

*Plus.* Where did she go ?

*Incia.* To get us food to eat.

*Plus.* Are you hungry, child ?

*Incia.* O dear, yes.

*Plus.* Where do ye live ?

*Incia.* O, we have come from afar off.

*Plus.* Where are ye going?

*Incia.* To London.

*Plus.* Are ye strangers ?

*Incia.* Yes; we were never here before.

*Plus.* Then I will lead ye safe to town. What cruel mother could leave her babes thus ? Ah, is this thy mother?

**Enter Boadicia.**

*Incia.* Yes.

*Plus.* Then will I approach her. Woman, are these thy children ?

*Boad.* They are, Roman; loose their hands'; they claim no protection from thee.

*Plus.* They are thy children, take them. (They go to their mother—she is about to turn and leave Plusso) Woman, let me persuade yon from this retreat; it is dangerous, damp, and ill becomes the place for health and infancy.

*Boad.* Where would yon lead us, Roman ?

*Plus.* To a quiet couch in a small villa in a sunny glen, beside the Thames, where ye can rest thy weary head, and close thy eye in that sweet sleep that shuts out the thought of busy life, and lets the soul in pleasure roam among the beauties of sweet dreams which draw us near to paradise.

*Boad.* Is there no danger in this pleasure Plus. Upon my life will I protect ye for the night, and guard ye at my own door, and feed thee at my own board with wine and meats, and guide thee after thy repast, safe to the town of London.

*Boad.* Thou speakest like a man of honesty; I'll follow thee.

*Plus.* A Roman locks not his door 'gainst hospitality.

*Boad.* Come, children. What noble kindness ! Unknowingly we speed our blessings with the things we hate, and that which we would best consume we but create, and leave a wonder to the world as choice as honey moon ! [Exit.]


ACT II.


SCENE II.—*A Street in London* A. D. 1—Temple of Diana —Senate House seen over the tops of others, in the distance— Market Place.

Enter two Romans, L.—Crimmerii, R.

*1st Roman.* Thou hast lied of me, told base falsehoods, and would me injure, and rob my private character.

*2d Rom.* No

*1st Rom.* Dost thou yet persist?

*2d Rom.* I do.

*1st Rom.* What argument have ye?

*2d Rom.* That thou for much selfish aims, would bring on self-abuse, in hope of sympathy.

*1st Rom.* O villain; I liar !

*2d Rom.* I am a Roman.

*1st Rom.* And I.

*"2d Rom.* Then should you show more patience and forbearance.

*1st Rom.* To thee ?

*2d Rom.* Why not ?

*1st Rom.* No; thou hast told base lies.

*2d Rom.* Me ?

*1st Rom.* Yes, knave.

*2d Rom.* (strikes him on the face.) Take that for thy redress.

*1st Rom.* Now have I thee with evidence.

*2d Rom.* This man saw I was provoked to such, and knows the conduct of such men as thou. I'm glad of such evidence; he is an honest man. (Market people gather.)

*1st Rom.* (to Crimmerri.) Saw you this man strike me? Did you not see him raise his arm against me ? Did he not smite me wilfully? Speak, thou wert a spectator.

*Crim.* I am no evidence in this case.

*1st Rom.* Did you not see him use violence on me ?

*Crim.* I saw him perform that good part that fools receive from the hand of wisdom; and ye, like a willing ass, stand choking down the bitter cud of sad experience, which sweetens in the stomach; which gives life and elasticity to common sense; which makes reason glorious and purifies the wit.

*1st Rom.* Insulting pigmy, feeder of swine, who wouldst thou rebuke ?

*Crim.* No one.

*2d Rom.* There is too much revelry for this early hour. Gentlemen, retire.

*1st Rom.* I'll meet thee in the chamber of the Senate, where we will have a different scene from this.

*2d Rom.* 'Tis well.      [Exit.]

*Crim.* If my wits do not deceive me, ye will have a much different scene from this.

*1st Rom.* Hush, thou servile thing; I'll raise thee so high from this gravelled earth, that ye'll grow dizzy with your exaltation.

*Crim.* Ah !

*1st Rom.* Ah, impudence ! I'll to the Senate go, and from the rostrum speak of this insult, to this effect: " Hang all base barbarians, that would our Roman's mock."

*Crim.* You ?

*1st Roman.* Aye, me !

*Crim.* A pig must squeel in paradise! Ha ! ha ! ha !

*1st Roman.* To be beaten and laughed at. I'll have redress ! [Exit.]

*Crim.* Poor paltry power; 'tis such asses as these that ye do clothe, then brand them men! Royalty, for shame to shoot at! O prudence, where are ye ?

*Market Woman.* Here, master !

*Crim.* Woman, to thy produce! give it thy reckoning oar, and calculate thy gains from usury. M. W. And ye did call me ? Crim. Woman, I named but Prudence. M. IF. Sir, and that is me.

*Crim.* Woman, I call'd not for but that sweet virtue that makes this world contain what little happiness man can enjoy, and harmonious all in love, without force or power. M. IV. Ah ! and who is Prudence, then ?

*Crim.* Prudence is a king. Power is but a slave.

*1st M. W.* Listen not to this stuff!

*2d M. W.* No, he is some fortuneteller. (All return laughing—Boadicia and Plusso appear, and children.)

*Crim* O tyrant ignorant ignorance ! O shame humanity! And yet, methinks there is more virtue in these unlettered shapes, sprung from so rough a soil to feast the appetite of manliness, than had they been fashioned up in Rome. Ah, Boadicia !

*Boad.* Oft the hand that would smother us is held for our support.

*Plus.* True, true !

*Crim.* Now must I aside for fear of recognition too soon. Yon tree must shield me in its shadow, or with the statue of Diana, and live a listening god.

*Boad.* For the small genius of material eyes sees not the object of the inner life—eternal.

*Plus.* Aye, I have looked deep into the arts of every science which the secrets of our nature has composed, and find all is doubt and vanity.

*Boad.* Use great discretion in every life, and ye will find more value in mankind than skepticism gives, which ye would call discretion.

*Plus.* Advise not that; for did we use too much discretion we would be a sober-minded set, and frighten off that welcome smile which gives toleration to our kin, and makes base man approachable.

*Boad.* True, true; but see the dial shift its finger hurriedly—and time is crawling fast upon us. Unless we proceed to our intent we will be late at the assemblage.

*Enter Page*

*Plus.* Yes—this Page of mine will lead thee there immediately. As I have other work in hand, I'll leave thee in his care.

*Boad.* Thanks, stranger, thanks !

*Incia.* Mother, when will we go home again ?

*Boad.* Tomorrow.

*Page.* With thy consent, I'll act the willing slave to truth and modesty, well meant.

*Plus.* Approach her boy: but remember, tamper not with riper age than thine; show reverence, not impudence; show courtesy, not fear. Go—I'll await thy coming in the senate chamber.　　[Exit.]

*Page.* It seems ye have your way mistook, as my master says. A stranger in London ! May my knowledge of this place lead up to safety and to good accommodation.

*Boad.* It may.

*Page.* Lady, thy name—I presume thou hast one ?

*Boad.* Yes—I have a name.

*Page.* And it is—

*Boad.* Not to be named at this place or time.

*Page.* Forgive me, lady, my impertinence, forgive ! (Aside.) This woman holds a secret. I'll swear by Jupiter she tells it before tomorrow eve. But I hate such women; for she a secret keeps, and looks on man suspiciously. Are you ready ?

*Boad.* Yes.

*Page.* Methinks this is the street.

*Boad.* Be sure, kind youth; let not presumption steal thee into error. My mission is most sacred; therefore, look well about thee, and wait not till thou art satisfied.

*Page.* I am sure !

*Boad.* The will is treacherous. They tell me from the home I've come that evil signs hang out in London Can ye read correctly?

*Page.* Yes—I am quite sure, indeed Ah!—yes, I read it now—it is a better place.

*Boad.* Proceed if thou art sure. I am thy guest in London, let come what will. (Romans pass.) How wears the customs here ?

*Page.* As all Rome wears — a custom disciplined, and quite befitting.

*Boad.* Then must I a more civil suit put on, and assume more enlightenment in my dress, if brains do not the part possess for inaugurating gods. (Pass a body of Romans.) Here seems to flow the purple cloth of favor most finely trimmed. How are these people dressed?

*Page.* To please the taste of Nero, great Emperor of Home.

*Boad.* Then I'll wear with them all of quality the same and see if better clothes hold higher laws than common sense, in Nero's name.

*Page.* Ha ! ha ! ha ! ye people from the country come look strange upon our city customs, and heap on your low-born happy state the finished troubles of the great, that sit on cushioned perfidy!

*Boad.* Child of Rome ! art thou so modest, then ? thou would'st not be as great as Roman gods assume. Thou art over-modest, boy !

*Page.* It is nonsense for a boy like me to assume the faults of modesty which woman should possess

*Boad.* Ah !

*Page.* It is her sword—her shield—her password—her freedom !

*Boad.* Ah ! How great! How beautiful!

*Page.* And the fine vine that grows above the pitfalls of deep sin, That youth with erring steps pass by unknowingly drop in !

*Boad.* Modest youth—how vainly cutting! I know the disposition of thy sex too well to offer such a bribe ! Thy soul is in thy hands; hold thou well on to it.

**Enter two Romans.**

*1st Roman.* A barbarous wench of Breton's street drags her filthy hands to London !

*2d Roman.* They tell you this is true.

*1st R.* Yea—great Plusso's pardoned her!

*2d R.* The weak-hearted Plussos?

*1st R.* Yea, she comes with the apology of protection for those wild Danes — those shaven-headed thieves ! She should be spit upon, and stoned beyond the city walls !— like pity when from home deserted !

*2d R.* But she is a woman !

*1st R.* O, we suppose !

*2d R.* True, she is supposed to be!

*1st R.* Perhaps the gender is not known among such wild boars of the west, that claim such privileged destiny.

*2d R.* Perhaps not. Ha, ha! perhaps decides it frequently ! See the good people gather in the market place ! Our curious brain adheres to wonder; perhaps they have her there. (Return up the stage.) 'Twill be a sight to see her!

*1st R.* What a woman ! Ha, ha !

*2d R.* Perhaps she be a woman—ha, ha, ha! [Exit.]

*Boad.* 'Tis well they saw us not. (Aside.) Are these Romans—these men ?

*Page.* Yea, peradventure, Romans.

*Boad.* Then lead on. I am convinced this is the public will. O, little sympathy must we expect that stand in bold misfortune's way. Now let wise thoughts my hopes caress! My life is ventured on this step ! Let Rome be Romans all —lead on !

For in these truths that cramp the air,

And fill the bosom with despair,

We see what other worlds possess.

And the insufficiency of this;

Where pains and sorrows too oft inspire

The suppliants to holy prayer !

*Incia.* Mother, are we going home now?

Load. No—to the citadel.

Locia. Dear mother ! O !—

*Boad.* Hush thy crying?, child ! Mother will protect thee!

[Exit.—Crimmerii advances]

*Crim.* To be an idle spectator of this world's doings; to watch and listen to mankind as he assumes and dictates to the impulses of a fevered brain, requires more coldness in the heart than the fair statue of Diana holds, rounded in that sweet form of virgin loveliness. Yes, Boadicia moves with god-like firmness, and points her talents to the issue of this dream, which, methinks, will interpret more truth than fiction, else I've no part to act, or hold no claim upon Anglesia's coronet. [Exit.]

## ACT II.

SCENE III—The Senate Room of London—Senate in sitting —Serestanus Paulaus in the chair.

***Serestanus Paulaus.*** Senators, thou art both in error. I am sorry that ye should assist in drawing on the troubles that surround us.

*1st R.* But I must have redress ? Must Romans suffer insult ?

*2d R.* Ha, ha, ha ! go hunt contentment for its shirt, and ye will find redress! The fowl flies home to roost! Ha, ha !

*S. Paul.* Roman, it is as I were told, that ye have fallen so far beneath the looks of good society that ye laugh at everything.

*2d R.* Then it is that I have become more wise, and, like a child, laugh at all that's silly ! My lords, I have no fur ther argument.         [Exit.]

*1st R.* Must we suffer this ? Must this bold man compromise us all ?

*S. Paul.* I will note this; yet we must use much courtesy with this aged Roman. As we would weave a garland for the ox when we would offer him a sacrifice, so place we a golden crown upon men's heads when we would steal their souls away.

*1st R.* This delay has hurried much rebuke, and makes men curse the good they hoped for, which thou withheld.

1st Senator. Yes, my lord, now is the cloud black upon us.

*S. Paul.* Now like trusty mariners must we evade the dangers of our ship, by giving to our troubled fright the firm belief of safety. So fear not; let the ship ride on. I'll to the helm. We'll save the ship in spite of circumstances. Pull ye stoutly to the oars.

*2d Sen.* My lord, where, you upon the lookout, and I from off the deck saw dangers in our course, could all thy promises persuade me of their innocence, unless the helm was put about, and we another course did take, though it were making hard in the wind's face.

*S. Paul.* I know, good gentlemen, the mind bears with all loose trash that fills the street, and often blinds the eyes of those whose duty calls them to face its fury. But I'll mind that.

**Enter Citizens, &c., with Crimmerii.**

There is too much meddling with affairs of state. Let every man be to his occupation pleased, keeping good conduct with good sense, and drop all curiosity as to affairs much foreign to their capabilities, for these sad attempts in vanity disgrace much greater deeds. If men would keep this world in peace, and make this nation's feast a paradise, as they oft expressed it so, let them forsake the envious devil of ambition that sports in every countenance;

Which makes the youths the gods may choose, Limp with yellow cheeks in old men's shoes.

**Enter a Tribune.**

Hold! here is something yet untold! Why this hurry? Speak ! slave, what is this ?

*Tribune.* With the rabble at yonder door stands a woman for admittance, in charge of Plussos' page.

*Plus.* Let her advance; she is my guest.

*2d Sen.* Who is this, Plussos ?

*S. Paul.* Down, I'll hear no debate.

*Enter Page, Boadicia, and children.*

*1st R.* My lord !

*1st Sen.* My lord !

*2d Sen.* My lord! I—

*S. Paul.*. Hold, ye babblers! what have we here ? This gives decision to our work. Here is a woman in much impudence. What phantom can this be ? Hold ! hark ! sit down !

*2d Sen.* Ye gods ! she is in her manner princely dressed, but in her look bears some strange wench much given to loose extravagance and shallow nothingness.

*S. Paul.* Down. We'll hear her.

*Boad.* These are the senators, I take it, and this the senate chamber. How nobly sit they to their seats—so godlike silent! There is much form in their administration, else they so circumspect would not assume the duty of high order, the first law of power. What splendor surrounds these demigods! Had they the virtues of their titles, they would not envy our low cots annd mean repast, but joyously construct this magnificence in our behalf, in honor of the gods that guide them. O, world of beauty, art, and honor ! how bright! how gay! how noble ! All this is from mai's favor, easier lost than memory. And this crowned slave is master of it all, who sits above the rest of men as if he were a king. This must be Serestanus, Nero's representative. Citizen, great thou art in thy position, or great thou would'st be, as ye assume. Thou can'st not close thy ears 'gainst mercy, else thou art not the man I'm seeking. I will before thee stand and offer my petition; come, children. Yet I fear refusal. Fear, what art thou ? Imp of cowardice, that would cheat me of a kingdom—avaunt!

(Advances toward senators.)

*S. Paul.* Ah, by heavens !—no,—

*Boad.* Most good and gracious master ! Noble and admired supreme ! exalted to thy nation's highest honors !

*S. Paul.* See these hounds lick dust for bread. A flatterer ! [Exit]

*Boad.* See before you a feeble woman; look down upon this weak hand that well supports a firm petition; see in myself my motive; see in this asking how great my need; see in my great fatigue how great my purpose. With my faith in Nero's goodness— (offers)—it's but a trifle which I ask. Take it, O, take it and read it! Take it, good master, and relieve my hand wherein I've held so tightly on since first I drew the resolution For mercy and my children, I do beseech you take it! O, take it—) (all kneel)—I pray thee here upon my bended knee;—and must I kneel so low ? Before no monarch have I ever knelt with half this courtesy!

*S. Paul.* Necessity makes humanity its tools, which proves much virtue in its severity.

*Boad.* O, I pray thee take it! Let not my labor waste to this; O take it!

*S. Paul.* Ha ! ha! ha !

*Boad.* (Rises.) What, laugh at me ? not speak to me ? No, no !

*S. Paul.* No—away; I knew ye not!

Boad Not know me ? O, lack the introduction; fault begets forgiveness. Great potentate !—a wondrous man ! So willingly forgetful ?—not know me ! Is this the small respect for greater earnings—not know me ? Was I not in sweet Icenia in-stalled ? Ah !—(S. Paul, recognizes her— great confusion in the senate.)

*Plus.* What—Boadicia !—and me—

*S. Paul.* How—a guest of Plussos !

*Boad.* Not know me ! Saw you not my husband falling in death ? Pledged you not his firmest friendship ? Offered you no compromise in his dying hours ? Was he not firm to thee in every promise ? How spoke ye then to him—of his wife and children, his people and his kin ? Have ye visited their huts since then ? No. Hast thy neglect betrayed thy memory ? Ah, know not me !—this is more torturing than abuse. Thy treatment has been cruel. We have mourned thy sad neglect, and many in our province preach their deep and trying wants that bate them on to infamy, which makes willing beggars of us all, for sake of honesty. And even my nearest kin are as bondsmen held, who complain and say this is hot liberty. It's something else; they know not what to call it yet. Must civilization teach such games as barbarity despises ? No, no ! If ye would men reform, and have them convinced of good, feed and clothe them, then preach and they'll believe,—not else. But in them noble men doth reign ignorance supreme, which seems a consolation and a friend, and keeps their minds in peace. But times are changing rapidly, and nations open wide their eyes and stare at this wondrous fear, and cry, Is this reform, refinement, and renown ? O, how hideous ! Then, since I have explained myself, an introduction given, thy memory recalled, accept my coming; my queer recital excuse; accept this parchment; in thy hand behold it; read it, and act the nobler part of man, dressed in much good authority. Take it, I pray thee, take it! No, no, thou wilt not take it!

*S. Paul.* Begone !—away! I hold no connection with thee. Slaves, show her the outer door ! Senate to order— heed not this!

*Boad.* Now comes our purpose to its fill.

*Crim.* Off, slaves!

*Boad.* Great gods ! that made us all, and gave us all the goods wherein we eat, drink, and wear, when made you up this man ? for why did form his mind to such queer things as this ? He—he who does despise his memory, treats kindly recollection with a mean contempt, and can forgive his own great evils remorselessly—he, this man ! Am I polite ? Recollect you that in my husband's dying did ye not send among our midst some wolves of thy own wearing, who from our rude cottage doors did drag our very sustenance, provoking our people to much bitter ire, as they were well to say to please good Nero with. How shall I note this goodness I No, no !

**S. Paul.** Woman, be careful; retire !

**Boad.** O, much warning and much scandal have I had since first I came to London. He that can his mother kill and smile upon her in her death, and call it beautiful !

**1st Sen..** Must we hear this ?

**S. Paul.** Silence !

**Boad.** He that can in passion kick into his wife a dread disease—a gentle, loving Octavia, as Romans named her. O, Poppea, polluted bitch, who named thee thus ? Poor Barrhus ! for all thy labor on this truant boy and thy friend Seneca, both men improper paid, and he, this thing, in man, perched on his golden throne, sings authority supreme. O, mockery ! O, shame ! O, hate ! O, contempt!

**2d Sen.** My lord, shall we not hear from thee ?

**1st R.** Stop this, or, by Great Jove, we will soon be at loose ends with all the populace !

**Boad.** Monarch ! tyrant! thou darest not speak; it's not your pleasure for excuse. Let fact be settled. O, blinded fool!—for I must call thee so—thou hast no face for knavery. What art thy wits about ? see not these people here about me ? I read that they arc pleased in this plain speech. Are ye so pleased I Was Rome in one grand conflagration ? Were gladiators pouring out their crimson life in circus rings, beneath the sweat and toil of damn'd excitement ? was persecution at its pleasing pitch ? Then would'st thou smile, aye, in honesty, repeat, Well done, good and faithful!

***S. Paul.*** Ha, ha, ha ! a crazy woman !

***Boad.*** Or wert thou with some loafish thing of stinking font to an altar hot for hymenal rites, bending your accursed head to vain deceit. These are thy soul's pleasures. O'er these thy mind is honest, and, ha, ha's boldly ! But when goodness comes to thee on its hands and knees to beg a trifle, with the white print of famine on the lip, you kick it down; but thou canst not kick me down. Great as thou art, or as thou wouldest be, I tell thee to thy teeth, I abhor thee. I hate thee now; from the bottom of my heart I hate thee ! O, thou despised of all the gods ! thou mean contempt of nature, when look ye for thy power ? Have ye made calculation ? Thou sophisticated spawn of hell, I leave thee to thy intoxications—farewell!

***S. Paul.*** Seize her, slaves ! Why stand you at this ? Can ye stomach all in blasphemy? Arrest her—bear her away.

Crim Hold! Off, slaves ! off, thou hirelings of a base ruler; lay not thy weight upon this flesh of woman ! Thy master's hands contaminate in touch; he has forsworn the virtues of a woman. Let her retire in peace; if not, I will descend like a mighty avalanche upon ye, and set thee at thy posts.

***Plus.*** And who is this ?

***Boad.*** O, great Plussos, a friend thou art, 'tis true; plead for me; correct my diction; purify my speech; so I may to the saints appeal in words appropriate for the laws of mercy, else I am lost for want of clear expression of the good I seek.

***Crim.*** 'Tis useless; there is no mercy in these men. S. Paul Who is this? Senator, (Who?), slaves, citizens, must we this insult bear?

*Sen.* and m-m. No, no !

*Crim.* Move not one step, (disguise fall off) *or by the holy bands that bind us to the laws of charity and self-defence, I'll thus enforce the arm of old Crimmerii.* (Great confusion—all surprised.) *Boadicia, retire.* (She retires slowly.)

*Boad.* Crimmerii—

*Crim.* Retire. Senators, I foresaw and knew all this from the oft practice which our habits give us to read men's cruelty, in these kindly offerings and promiscuous promisings of such men as ye. Nero and ye are cousins in infamy; the harness fits you both. We shall meet again, I hope. Farewell.   [Exit, much excited]

*Tri.* Ho, the guard, the guard ! Sound the alarm ! (Bells toll.)

*S. Paul.*. (Rushes from his seat.) O, O, what is this that I have tasted ?

**Enter Generals, Tribunes, &c., in confusion**

Ho, haste the inarch for base Anglesia. Bring me my sword and buckler, I'll mount the expedition with myself. (To generals—drums beat and flourish of trumpets.) *Ho, haste to thy quarters immediately; number thy choicest men. I fear the power of this unlettered force. O, vengeance, vengeance cheats diplomacy, and substitutes excuse for haste, which leads us to empires and renown, while cold formality would settle down consistency for both, and rob us of our prize which we so long have sought, but wanting provocation. To arms ! to arms ! to vengeance and renown !* (Curtain falls—soldiers fill the chamber—with music, &.c.) To arms !

# ACT III.

SCENE I.—Scene in Anglesia, by the river — Romans seen landing in the distance from barges—Country wild and romantic—Boadicia's chariot standing waiting for her—Barbarians armed with spears, bows, pikes, &c.

*Enter Boadicia, her chiefs, daughters, priests, &c.*

*Soldiers.* Hail, the queen, the queen !

*Boad.* Friends, be quiet. Thy hollow hootings are but scare freaks to thy native courage. Retain thy sober thoughtfulness, and keep thine eye well fixed upon the records of thy fates, for sorry news is this I bring from London.

*Crim.* (The banner of characters is brought forward.) Within this circle plant we our standard. Around this draw we the bands of union. Here suffer we with every fate; alike exact in every favor, and hold unto ourselves a common suffering, and hold obedience to the council of thy will. Can volumed threats provoke us more ? have we not suffered all in forcing toleration ? We smiled at insult, laughed at want, and hushed our indignation. Have we not proven the lowliness of our condition in meek obedience and silent tongue ?

*All.* Yes, yes, yes !

*Crim.* Are we not baffled in every effort which asked for peace ? Ah, sorry turned the scale, and we could see thee limping home with hope deep sunken in the eye, and pulse that beat with milky streams; for we could see thee white with fear, through unnoticed dignity. Thus have we well prepared your home reception, and paved it with good feelings from the souls of men that live on inspiration in thy sight, and die when thou art gone. Thy presence is immaculate. Can the lily bloom without its sun ? No; nor can man assume without his hope. Thus draw we noble souls for noble deeds. Who deign to kiss the earth 'less glory sweets it, and claim of honor life's ill in the eye of death an equal portion ? Convictions of our weakness rob us not for the attempt of justice.

**Boad.** Now let the public eye descend. Now let the mind appreciate its every expectation. See ye not the landing of yon host, with many legions filled with the intent of death and fame's high heraldry ? Is this peace—this protection—this kindness? O, sorry, sorry thought! Thus seem we shut in; about us hangs a deep misty air that stifles breath from fear, and wraps us all with dread, contrasting, as all horrors do, sympathy and shame. Are ye all asleep to death ? Awake, awake ! list to this proclamation; for I have sworn the issue such with much consideration. To war ! to war! to war! Aye, this would prompt the gods to battle. Such is thy alternative, such thy hope, relieving thy homes from the iron grasp of egotistical insanity, cloaked in bigoted humanity, that lord it over us with that base impunity of a sickening fury, to whom meekness grants authority. Can ye see all this and not complain ? Will ye let conceit fatten them in power? No, no ! (All shout.) *O, Rome, Rome! O, enlightened hell, where hold ye this claim on us ? Where got ye consent to fasten to our flesh this burning sore ? Would we give ye all confidence ? No, no, we would as soon trust Pluto with the keys of Paradise as give thee such submission. Men of my nativity, where are ye ? To arms ! to arms ! Look out on yonder shore; see ye no enemy ? Look to yon wedded hill; see ye no cottage home ? hear ye not the tramp of death ? feel ye not the beatings of warm hearts ? ask none for protection ? To arms ! Your widowed queen bids ye to arms, to arms !* (shouts.) *Look ye for monuments of fame; look when tradition gives a name with gold-laced sandals tipped. " Caroctacus," see what bold strides this hero made; see all his steps in jewels laid, for his redress on Rome. Fear not, posterity will do the homage. Shake off thy native sleepiness; open wide thine eyes to thy responsibility, and let this world of wonder know how glorious Britain fares. Show well the men she owns. Show all how nature has ye formed to suit its oft conveniences, which raised ye to the aim of men in all its bold supremacy. How excellence with time has formed what hope from beanteous talents caught. How men with minds of valor can sustain the honors of the great, by proving worth for woman. Away,* *unto thy clans repair. Let courage guard good feeling. Let hope illume thy heavy brow; for from this place I do declare the world is all at war. Away, thy country calls thee to the field. Let family altars be thy shields, thy recompense, thy gods. Away! to arms ! away!* (Exit all in order—Boadicia mounts the chariot with her two daughters) Onward to glory—on ! [Exit.]

**Enter Comos and Alanthus.**

*Alanthus.* See, Comos, are there no signs ?

*Comos.* No.

*Alan.* Are there no voices ? Hark! methinks the troubled air is filled with a strange sound.

*Comos.* Are the Beacons answering ?

*Alan.* Ah, (look to the ships) see, see, Comos—how beautiful ! The sails, bent gently to the towering masts, fill slowly with coming air, and bear them smoothly toward the leeward shore.

*Comos.* Who—who ?

*Alan.* The sign is Roman.

*Comos.* Then come we to the issue of our work, or, I should say, the beginning of the end; for all these discordant sounds which long have filled our cars with fear and hesitation, will by these instruments be tuned to such fine airs as make the mind more happy in its time of death, with hope for its key-note, than life with all its (amby pamby) strain within the key of shame, with fear and sorrow for master poets. Roman, welcome! for in thy issue is death or victory. Let the die be cast for both of us, but one must win. Shuffle on—the stakes are up !

*Alan.* Comos, be not so sad, so long-faced; speak not so oft of death—so oft of troubles.

*Comos.* Alanthus, 'tis thy place to be always gay. I am much oppressed in business of thought, and then you seem so sad when I am but in thought.

*Alan.* But when thou art with me, ye should be gay, as I am happy most when ye most seem so. Set aside thy meditations,

*Comos.* Then be happy. Ha, ha, ha! for I will laugh, too —ha, ha !

*Alan.* Comos, that is not happiness.

*Comos.* Why, it seems ye thought so; ye say I do not laugh.

*Alan.* All are not happy that give vent to volumes of laughter.

*Comos.* No, much sorrow mingles in every joy. Shadows follow sunshine; so in the noble minds of men we oft do see the light of knowledge burning in the eye with that pure grace, the nobility of thought, which the calm water represents when we upon its bosom sail, casting our weak sight down, down, deeper, through its transparent tide as it moves gently on above deep buried pearls that shine so pure, so chaste, so calm, so bright, so holy, like burning sapphire that stud the heavens, which above us hang like one broad covering of a majestic mind over man supreme, reposed, calm, refined, and thoughtful!

*Alan.* Ah, who is this ? My Comos !

*Comos.* A babbling brook—that gives all joy but in Expression, and sounds all happiness on the lip. True thought is true joy. A great mind langhs with charity—a shallow skull with ridicule. A great mind comments with greatness—a weak mind with contempt and foolery, and criticises when it should praise.

*Alan.* How shall I ever be happy ?

*Comos.* Be good; have charity, kind thought. But ah, see, the advance is upon us. We must haste away, else my absence will be noticed. Come, Alanthus, with me to the camp.   [Exit.]

*Enter Sercsterns Paulanus and his army.*

S. Paid. Halt!

*Enter officers.*

§ [ *1st Off.* My lord, we are in hot pursuit; for as we arose yon eastern hill we plainly saw the whole of Boadicia's army.

*S. Paul.* How many, strong ?

*1st Off.* From spies which we well bribed by coins and threats, two hundred thousand strong.

*S. Paul.* Two hundred thousand !

*1st Off.* So say these men. If they do lie it's much against their policy and their priestcraft.

*S. Paul.* Priestcraft is policy. Then am I stronger in the field than I had thought. Poor savage queen ! Poor Boadicia, thy very face but arguments thy defeat. Undisciplined, unused to customs carved by sharpened steel, how can ye suffer all ? But I must advance, and by tomorrow's sun shall by this blade I draw tell how the chances run. Advance !     [Exit all.]

***Re-enter Alanthus.***

*Alan.* Thus am I compelled from the rude camp to fly for fear the shafts of war with little grace may pierce my virgin brerst. 'Twas Comos' wish that I should retire. Ah, but no, no ! I cannot go afar, for I do hold some strange presentiments in my mind, which embody forth much fear.

For on yester eve, as I was sitting by the window of my rustic cot, a little bird came winging to my side with a solemn chirp, as if the evil sorrow of mankind held power on its life. It seemed so weary in the wing, which by our forms portends much evil. Hark! ah! list! list! [Exit.]

***Enter Paulos and Camperi.***

*Camp.* Hold, Paulos; we have retreated far enough.

*Paul.* How stand they now ? O, that I had remained in peace !

*Camp.* Ah, they fly !

*Paul.* Who—the Romans?

*Camp.* No, the Bretons.

*Paul.* O, heavens protect us ! O, O, O !

*Camp.* No, no, it is—ah, the Romans speed all over the-nill like frightened sheep—ah, they fly, they fly!

*Paul.* Ah, yes, yes, the day is ours. Ho, Camperi, let's to the field again !

*Enter Comos.*

*Comos.* Men, why art thou here ? This is not the field which chiefs employ—why art thou here?

*Camp.* I came with Paulos, that we might from this summit gain a more advantageous view, and mark the progress of our clan, as they nobly beat the wolves away from our happy folds.

*Comos.* If valor prompted thee to war, honor should have held thee in the field, and saved thy character. Thy queen has missed thee; go and explain thy absence.

*Paul.* Did she seem offended ?

*Comos.* No.

*Camp.* When missed she us ?

*Comos.* When the battle first began we noticed your clans inactive; on regaining we found you were away. So summoning two noble fellows of thy flock, commissions were to them conveyed, and they within the hottest broil turned aside the fatal shaft of war, and gave our queen the victory, which honor they received.

*Camp.* O, Paulos, thy fear has robbed me—ruined me for ever—farewell. [Exit.]

*Paul.* Friend Comos.

*Comos.* Call me no friend. Away and seek thy pardon for thy guilty soul. Thy friendship breathes on cowards.

*Paul.* I'll to the queen.

*Comos.* Go. I held thee once in much esteem, but since I've found thee afraid to die methinks thou art not worthy of the pride I held in thee. Thus is man sacrificed to fear. Thus is good honor lost on hesitation. O, man, if thou art the pattern, wherein is prompted every good divinity controls, why do ye mock yourselves in the low conceits that guide the impulses of the wicked mind, and run with quickened speed into the precipice of death that dashes thee with maddening fury against the gates of hell, art thou not conscious ? With little effort and good mind, how quick we blow to favor ! and backed by popularity and a good name, we could circumnavigate the world in glory, installing man in every excellence, and making him not what he is, but change his sufferings to scenes of joy, and give him wings of royalty, beneath whose shadows virtue lives, and hope in peace reposes. (An arrow falls by him.) Ah, thou barbed messenger of ruder times, why hail me in my revery ? Is the battle up again ? Ah, yes—the strife. See, they move to action; Comos, to the field again! (An arrow strikes him—he staggers as he leaves the stage.) O, what is this ? The first was harmless, a forerunner of fate; this— it reels my brain; it staggers on my sense; I feel a heaviness within my skull; my blood seems thickening in my veins! O, is this death—death! Alanthus, Alanthus! how oft is man baffled when his hopes are highest; how most deceived when he most perseveres ! No, no ! she shall this wound bind up, and I will live in spite of death, and battle with the brave. Alanthus—Alanthus, or I die ! Life, what art thou? Ambition, what art thou ? Courage, valor, victory, where are ye now ? O, death, ye have no charity, no regard for all man's hope ! Alanthus, Alanthus ! [Exit.]

## ACT III.

### SCENE II. — *A Wooded Scene in Wales.*

**Enter Boadicia and Garbolos and suites.**

*Boad.* Thus far has prosperity allured us. Without impediment have we installed the fear we first proposed, and stamped upon the Roman brow the horrors of defeat, who boisterously into our land did march with officers well disciplined, to bind us down to shame. But by the good arm which Andate guides, we have the odds much overthrown and left them in much vexation and chagrin, from defeat so unexpected; which to us all much animation gives, from the encouragement of success, which cheerfully in peace will guide the issue of this chance at war

***Garb.*** Thy words burn in our cars, illuminate the soul, and make us warm again wherein we had coldly grown.

### *Enter Crimmerii and Chiefs.*

***Crim.*** London, St. Albans and Caulanford have fallen! The enemy is crowding close upon our rear, and threaten battle instantly ! We must prepare and meet him with our weapons levelled at his heart!

***Boad.*** Great King—ye in your hurried message give much consolation and advice, which from the heart of which it springs, sounds nobly forth unto our minds, with much belief and satisfaction! London, St. Albans and Canlanford have fallen ! Glory spreads itself before us, and victory crowns us with its wreath afresh at every effort, that we may walk in honor's path, unto the throne of grace. Thus tyrants suffer by tyrant's laws.

Who institutes the blade of steel,

By which every monarch must a monarch feel!

Enter Officer—(to Crimmerii)

Office). My Lord, the enemy do press us hard along the left bank that skirts the Dee. We are much cut! Unless assistance soon does come, no force can this breach fill up. Our carelessness has made way for in its oversight of safety !

***Crim.*** Thus has succcss o'er flattered us, and when we thought ourselves so safe ! Rome, with a cunning eye saw at a glance all our weak assurance.

*Enter Officer.*

*Officer* 1. My Lord, I speed to tell that Camperi has fled!

*Enter Officer.*

*Officer* 2. My Lord, great Comos is dead !

*Enter Officer.*

*Officer 3.* My Lord, your daughter raves a maniac, and seeks among the enemy the slayer of good Comos! Crim. O ye gods, support me

*Enter Officer in hot haste.*

*Officer 4.* My Lord, I crave your help immediately, else victory will do us more harm than defeat, with all its fear, and courage, which a day ago knew us as heroes of the field, will know us no more forever!

*Boad.* My lords, attention ! Ho, to the field ! The tide of battle sways hard upon us, and fates do seem to pull withal 'gainst promises so flattering. (Enter Officer.) Halt! What news have ye—good or bad ?

*Officer* 5. Bad news, your grace! Lord Paulos has fled! Camperi is against us, and lights a lion, where he played the ass!

*Boad.* Camperi with Luistanus ! Why, he was among the first to swear allegiance to our cause ! He, traitor ! Poor promised man ! No sooner pledged than compromised by thy own consent. But come—when friend assumes the blade, let confidence supply a victim, and mark which issue fate will bring—the god traitor or the traitor king!

[Exit all.]

Enter Alanthus, a Maniac.

*Alan.* Comos, Comos—list, list—hark! Comos, ah, I see him. Comos, ah, list—ho, Comos dead, dead! Ha, ha, ha! Comos, list, list! (Music, sings)

We know not, we care not,

We feel not this pain,

That hears not, that sees not,

But robs this poor brain

Of reason's bright light!

It loves not, it fears not,

It goes not away;

It lives not, it dies not,

It makes our best day

A perpetual night!

### Enter Roman Officers.

Ah, disturb me? Men—no, ye are not men! Fiends, that rob me ! Where is my Comos ? Comos, bring back my Comos. O, ye fiends, why do ye so distract me?

Comos—Comos—where is he ? O where is he ? List, list, list—I hear him—yes, yes, he calls me ! Comos—Comos, I will come ! Yes, yes—no! (Officers approach her.)

Roman. This woman crazy seems; the trials have so estranged her brain, that she has crazy grown, and holds but little privilege in this reasoning world. Woman, woman—

*Alan.* List, list—Comos, Comos—hark, yes.

*Rom.* Woman—how

*Alan.* Release me, man; away, away from me; ye burn me with hot iron ! Away—help—help! Comos, Comos— Ah, list, list—he comes; he comes! List—he calls me! Alanthus; I come—I come ! List, list—yes, yes—I come, I come ! [Exit, slow and tearful.']

*1st Rom.* Thus have we the misfortunes of savage haste; the evils and fates of war.

*2d Rom.* Life's happiest bloom, pluck'd wits first blossoms.

**Enter Roman Officer.**

*1st Rom.* How sways the affairs of battle, when yc escaped the field?

*3d Rom.* We are in close pursuit; we broke the line; they fly, they fly—the day is won—the victory is ours !

**Enter S. Paulaus.**

*S. Paul.* Brave officers of Rome—congratulations must be brief, for we have got the heels of time and followed up the chance so well that we shall change the face of life and make the afIairs of this wide world assume, from this late hour, a different aspect for tomorrow's sun, which this fatal blow has sanctioned. The Queen does fly—the field is ours, With but a score of Rome, have we made way through Britain and the kingdoms !

***Enter Officer.***

***4th Rom.*** My Lord, the Queen has flown again.

***S. Paul.*** Sound the pursuit, (trumpet) —the chase is now in full! (Legions of Romans pass and repass.) Give them the lash of Rome ! Now is our compliment returned—now are the gods of war at ease—now is the story told; for Boadicia has turned tracks and holes herself for safety. (Enter Officer.) Found ye yet the Queen? How looks she? No!

***6th Officer.*** No, my lord, she escaped our grasp miraculously. We thought we saw her and did beat our foes with double fury to obtain her; for we knew the honor which it would confer, knowing she was the prime mover of the whole! But when we came wherewith she stood, she was not there; for she had flown on seeing our intent.

***S. Paul.*** Whither?

***6th Officer.*** No trace of her remains. Were she a myth and given to existence among the clouds, she could not sooner the transit made than did she in this circumstance.

***S. Paul.*** Her Children?

***6th Officer.*** They are victims of the camp. They were to worthy Scrope's hands installed, with many cautions as to their care, that they all tenderness should be shown, for they are of Boadicia born.

*S. Paul.* Aye, that was poor advice to Scrope, for he has paced the field in double honor, yet holds no compliment so high as the fair smiles of lovely woman, which has oft greeted his success. Saw you aught of king Crimmerii ?

*6th Officer.* He is in chains—a prisoner !

*S. Paul.* How ?

*6th Officer.* He offered no resistance in the fight, when we encountered him, and like a child, over sick with pleasure, he handed up his arms, like idle traps, saying, they were of little value now; I am done with them; take them, they are yours.

*S. Paul.* Bring him before me. [Exit Officer] Ye gods, what has so altered this great man—this King—this man of power ?

Enter Crimmerii and Officer—Crimmerii advances.

*Crim.* Ye have a right to all command; I obey.

*S. Paul.* Crimmerii, where's thy Queen ?

*Crim.* I know not.

*S. Paul.* Upon thy honor?

*Crim.* Upon my honor.

*S. Paul.* Crimmerii, why didst thou surrender ?

*Crim.* My Lord, why should I longer fight ?

*S. Paul.* Had ye no hope?

*Crim.* No hope! He is a fool that hopes in folly.

*S. Paul.* Then there must be an object in thy surrender, for ye had much confidence in battle, and like a fierce beast devoured all that came in thy way.

*Crim.* My Lord, summoned ye me for inquiry, to gratify and make me serve the envious questionings of an angry brain ? I am thy prisoner, not thy slave. Does not these chains identify my bondage? Let them smile that know no sorrow; let them chastise that bear no blame. For me, I have great share of both. And as to my intentions, they are innocent. A brave man gives his word, not for doubts, but for belief, which my position will justly with much truth.

*S. Paul.* How ?

*Crim.* Why should I more hold out ? Is not the day ended when the sun goes down ? Is not the summer ended when the winter comes ? Can the eye discern its beauty in the night? Can roses bloom when earth is white with frost? No ! Then what or whyfore should man live when hope is vanished from his soul—when ambition mocks him with its defeats, and war, the cruel monster which ye bestride, like some huge reptile of a demon world, aroused and bridled at your command, to ride unmindful o'er truth and justice, which robs him of all this world made dear—which savored life with sweetened toils, and made the little troubles which joy is heir to, but pastime for the intervals of joy?

*Home* —I have none ! No friends. Look out on yonder field, ye'll see how firm they were in their affections! The Queen—whither she has gone I know not. Andate has fallen, which alone decides our ruin. My wife—O, God— stop this thought! My child—my child ! Fiends, bring me my child! O, is there a God in heaven to witness this, and offer no redress ? Why torture me with shame? Why curse my child in all her purity? O, give me back my child—I say, my child I want!

*Enter Alanthus.*

*Alan.* Let me go—oh, let me go—it is my father ! Father !

*Crim.* **Alanthus** *!* (Embrace.)

*Alan.* What is this—where am I, father ?

*Crim.* Alanthus, my child !

*Alan.* These chains—these men! Ah, list—ah, he calls me!

*Crim.* Oh, what horrors crowd upon me! A maniac! No! Do my eyes deceive me ? Alanthus—Alanthus !

*Alan.* List, list, list!

*Crim.* What, my child, not know me? Alanthus !

*Alan.* I hear him? he calls, he calls—Alanthus, Alanthus !

*Crim.* Whither will ye ? Stray not from me. Who is it ye hear ? Who calls ?

*Alan.* Father, kiss me.

*Crim.* Fondly—there !

*Alan.* Father, I have much uneasiness of mind. Am I worthy, father, of one kindness ?

*Crim.* Yes, my child, all.

*Alan.* Father, list, list! Hark—it is past!

*Crim.* Alanthus, what means this?

*Alan.* Father, wilt thou forgive me ?

*Crim.* Was I ever ungrateful, Alanthus, my sweet child.

*Alan.* Never—but, oh, father

*Crim.* Speak, child, I forgive thee.

*Alan.* Wilt thou not be angry at me ? List, list, ah !

*Crim.* Thy father's word for it, I will not be angry— speak !

*Alan.* Not if I question thee ?

*Crim.* No.

*Alan.* List, list! Father, where is Comos—oh, where is he ? Comos, my life, my love !

*Crim.* My child, Comos is dead !

*Alan.* (shrinks.) Dead—dead! O, speak not of death! Life, what is thy inducements—why encounter me thus ? Fear, where art thou, now Comos is dead I O fate, why press me thus ? Dead, dead, dead !

*Crim.* O that I could have avoided this! Alan. Father, I thank thee. Father, forgive me. I am myself now—it is past! I go in peace! Kiss me once again ! Farewell—

farewell! Comos, I come to thee ! Father, farewell! (Dies.)

*Crim.* Farewell! Go, happy soul—go where ye will find more peace.' Thus have I seen them all depart! Ye gods, guide her and protect her—farewell! Now, tyrant, I am ready. Dispose of me as ye desire. I have no fear of death; for as ye see, I hold it near my heart, aye, in my own person do I support it, as the last and most lovely thing this earth and thy ill-will has left me. Are ye done with me ?

*S. Paul.* Soldiers, lead them away.

*Crim.* Now is my office filled—now have I the little part performed, which life has given heir to. Never yet was cause more holy why men should battle with contending ill, yet fate so curiously construed, renounce it. And from the efforts which the heart was with. We reap our rule in ruin. Tyrant, on with thy enlightened scheme, for power and possession! Thou, backed by deception and steel, are not so fearful as the troubled brain, which must its conscience oft consult, and find rebuke when it most promised praise. Ha, ha, ha! Howl on ye curse of Rome! Thy hope is too undone for good in ending is but began. Ha, ha, ha! O, Rome. Rome: why mock us with thy inference? Thus, tyrant, may ye well receive the curse ye did to freedom give, to stop the cause of Liberty!

[Exit Crimmerii, Alanthus and Guards.]

*S. Paul.* Keep this man from harm; give him attention. I hold no blame for him. "He is a man !"

*1st Rom.* Yet in in his speech, he did ye much abuse.

*S. Paul.* The speech of most men condemn more than inform. Believe not all ye hear; men speak from various causes. Now, where has this savage woman gone ? A mother and a friend; no common bounds can chain her will. She, who has this mighty army raised with all their native superstition, and given to all Rome a look of horror; she, who has met Paulanus face to face, upon the battle field, with equal will and bravery; she, who, like Cassandra of Troy, did send such prophetic fury among her clans and rile into their breasts this memorable issue—this decided fate—now, where has this woman gone? Defeated, fled !

### Enter a Legion of Roman Soldiers.

Is this all that's left to feast our Roman pride upon ? The trophy cost its value, yet we possess it not! Bring forth my swiftest chariot; I'll hunt this woman out, and see if all her deeds possess the virtues of a mind!

Enter Chariot and Horses—Scrostus mounts.

My people were my charge; I gave them all my power to this day. To cancel the deeds which will immortalize, not degrade. In acting duty's part, I hold no hate for Boadicia. I act my master's will: "Subdue them or annihilate!" I have done neither yet. But to this purpose I am resolved: I shall not rest this head again 'till Boadicia dies! The time wears on; let's to victory, endorsing by our bold acts the documents of Rome, long argued in our favor. Let's enroll our names in glory!

And Fame, the fire-eyed meteor which above us hangs,

Will give us power for our battle pangs! Away!

[Exit all, in good order.]

Barbarians enter and pass in much fright—Enter Garbolos.

*Garb.* All is lost, except this little life, so financed in its diet and resources, that to possess it is of more expense than heaven ever could recompense with twice ten thousand sighs, in penances and pardons. Yet must we bear with it all and suffer with all kin alike subject to death and mercy.

A life in mourning is a life most dear,

But evening shuts the shades in fear;

And night, when sleep and death do come,

Which guides us gently to the tomb!

Is what we most dread; yet for sweet slumber's sake, we take hand in hand and oft in heaven wake! How beautiful ! Would that I could so live, so sleep, so dream, so wake forever with the gods, free from this sorry world and its infirmities: for all is lost; the army and the queen Would that I could lose myself, not knowing what I've been, least I should find myself again in old Langolan's plain. For all is lost, lost, lost! All which teazed life with its anxieties is gone, gone, gone!  [Exit.]

***Enter Priests, with Asses. &c.***

*1st Priest.* Tut for the world's opinion.

*2d P.* But it brings power.

*1st P.* Where is the happiness of power—where its heart?

*2d P.* Why, in possessions.

*1st P.* It breeds more fear, more hate, more envy and more danger than our profession holds, backed by false constituency.

*2d P.* It brings renown.

*1st P.* It brings censure.

*2d P.* It gives command.

*1st P.* It gives contempt.

*2d P.* It begets honor.

*1st P.* It begets shame,

*2d P.* Then what is all this world so mad upon; which sounds so smooth so pleasing to the ambitious ear, and looks so charming to the expectant eye, and muses so fondly with the anxious mind—is it not the hope, the pleasure of power ? Are we not candidates for its cares ?

*1st P.* We are deluded by its surface; for it holds higher those that lightly sit; who crow, like the morning cock, when he ascends the highest; as if none before him reached the dung-hill of popular fame, o'er which he flaps and flaps his glossy wings with lordly circumspection; then hops he down to earth again, much wearied with the toils of his ascension, which, for a change, friend Olas, is not unhealthy to the pride.

*2d P.* Ah, friend Carols, I can see a more valuable insertion in the meaning of this word of power than ye can see.

*1st P.* I see it as a phosphoric light, evolving its fascinations with its deceit, from its own rottenness. A green and pleasing lawn, fair to look upon, pleasing to the eye, with biling adders crouched beneath its green and slippery paths, so beautiful; a bower of roses above a death morass, which, if we reach to pluck, we find the thorns are sharpest near the bloom, and crumbling quicksands play about our feet. A calm unrippled stream, with the full sun's rays bestowing heaven's mirror on its breast, while slimy vermin crawl at its depth, in all their native element, revealing horror and disgust!

*2d P.* But what is this ye show me ?

*1st P.* Two sides to power.

*2d P.* No man can relate unless he has experience had. 1st P. Experience is the cap for fools. Wisdom teaches with much higher rules, and shows the mind which can best appreciate the faults of flesh, which lie contagious to the virtues of the great; who most do power show, not from fear, but the base contaminations which to position adhere, in laws of present day.

*2d P.* Why, Carols, ye are more of philosopher than priest.

*1st P.* Then if ye will allow me to use philosophy between us: I think it good policy and both good philosophy if we would make our absence known unto this place, for there is changes in the scene, and we'll be caught without much ceremony, and loose our crowns to Roman pride, instead of a fat profession.

*2d P.* Then if there be danger in our stay, let's jog along towards our home, the Meni.

*1st P.* Buckle up thy girt and we'll be off. That's an honest pride that works for self.

*2d P.* Sure.

*1st P.* Then all is ready ?

*2d P.* Yes.

*1st P.* Follow: I'll lead the way back to the circles of our fathers, where we at easy games, can play with these men's tastes; like a growing famine in a nation's eye, which bids us from the good retreat, with evil well assuming, and muse the causes which festers sore within the breast of Rome, the mistress of the world, where power orders splendor, and splendor with its poisoned claims, robs man of much claimed freedom, and makes him, not a Roman freeman, but a Roman slave. Aye, I would sooner starve on bitter acorns and sour herbs, among the uncouth passes of our native hills, and be a monk withal, and sleep in savage caves, and call it freedom, than live a titled bondsman among the high of Rome. Who feast the honey from the comb, who hold the gudgeon of authority, and rest on feathered down, yet in the heart with black intent, riles up the shame of misgovernment, which they with sober looks presume will be Rome's profit from the faults of Rome? But will it prove so ? No.

For from this shore shall fredom spring,

The child of purity,

And claim for Britain, truth, the Lion, King.

To all posterity.  [Exit.]

***End of Act IT.***

ACT III.

SCENE III.—A deep, dark Cave—Enter Boadicia, cautiously and majestically, L.

***Boad.*** Hark, what strange sounds yet perch upon my ear, alluring me back to earth, as cautiously I tread into another world. I would be silent in my grief, therefore seek I out this unfrequented pass, free from the vulgar sight of man. The damp soot that smuts the air about this cave, half stifles in my breast the desecrations which I charge 'gainst men and their hypocrisy. But, let that pass. Where I, to use the vocabulary of this world, I do find it much too weak for the expressions which I seek from out the feelings of a heart so basely trodden on: yet will I stay my time to my own liking. 'Tis a nobler sight to see one's life plucked from its body in the health of thought, by its own consent, than linger out this little space on hope and borrowed chanty, Yes, in this deep abyss of earth, black with the contagions of dread night, will I reveal the power which to me remains above the laws of Rome. Here will I seal the seal of death, and save estate and gain attention to the end; for death is better than rebuke. Rebuke is the offspring of envy: death goes clothed in its divinity! Yes, here with this little antidote will I relieve this dreaded epidemic, and purge this world of that weak shame that rests in Boadicia. (Drinks) For why should I live to age ? Life! what is life on earth ? It is but a pastime for the heart to acquaint its soul with sin: it is but a brazen symbol, beaten by the prong of selfishness, which reverberates at every touch and sounds most loud when ye but tap it lightly; all shallowness and sound. A beautiful summer's morn to some, with placid pleasing balms to soft the senses to repose; while the great god of eastern day smiles forth in morning excellence, to give fresh vigor to the soul and make the passions bloom like sweetened tints that spot the jewelled lawn, from whose sweet dews comes heavenly fragrance to the eager sense. Ah, such a life I saw in youth; but chastening clouds soon dark the sun, and he may set without again returning the sweet smile which morning blessed ye with. So did he set, and all the beauty which from him caught life; fell gently from its sweetened bloom into the sombre arms of death. So let me die, To die— aye, that was the purpose of my birth. (Drinks.) Now the last drop is drained—now the last effort made which must redeem me from the bonds of Rome. Anglesea, farewell ! Britain, farewell! My children—O, my children ! O, ye gods, where have ye disposed of them ? Protect them; for in this time I am much lost, and have no power left to fathom back into the sinks of earth. Ye gods, take them to thy care ! Teach my memory! Farewell! What, is this death—death ? No! Yet it must be, for I have given it consent! This dreamy sense—this circling world— aye, my sight grows dim with it all! Where am I ? Ah, yes, I feel my freedom now! I feel earth's passing vanities! Death— death—O, death, what art thou—wherefore will ye take me —when or where ? Ah, no ! Now in the resolution of extremes must I show forth the power which the just contain in arguments of truth; that truth, though born in humble mien, and contents itself itself with right alone, is better for the souls of men than error in its positions claimed, with its responsibilities. My children—O, then 'tis past!

Farewell! Thy mother's blessing be on ye ! I would not inhale affection's fear to baffle resolution, for much exertion have I spent to guide the soul to this effect; by thwarting the efforts of weak life, with all its perquisites of hope; that I in peace must thus resign myself to death, and calmly watch the closing scene that sanctions every destiny. Yes, yes—I see. I see! My country! The Gods and Liberty! (Dies.)

The Cave disappears and Rome is seen in the distance, with Romans and the Sciences with civilization on one side, while Barbarians in their notice representation, are seen on the other —the Spirit of Boadicia rises among the clouds and disappears.

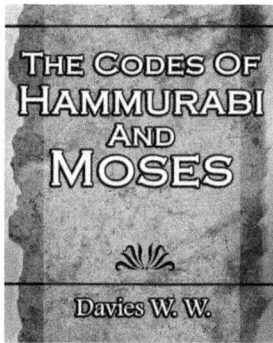

### The Codes Of Hammurabi And Moses
### W. W. Davies

QTY

The discovery of the Hammurabi Code is one of the greatest achievements of archaeology, and is of paramount interest, not only to the student of the Bible, but also to all those interested in ancient history...

**Religion** **ISBN:** *1-59462-338-4* **Pages:132**
*MSRP $12.95*

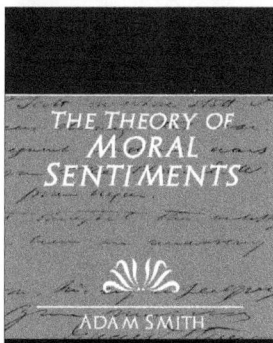

### The Theory of Moral Sentiments
### Adam Smith

QTY

This work from 1749. contains original theories of conscience amd moral judgment and it is the foundation for systemof morals.

**Philosophy** **ISBN:** *1-59462-777-0* **Pages:536**
*MSRP $19.95*

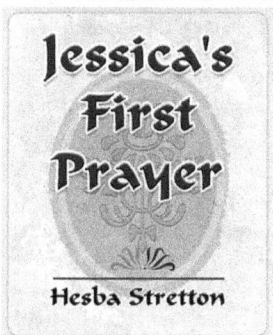

### Jessica's First Prayer
### Hesba Stretton

QTY

In a screened and secluded corner of one of the many railway-bridges which span the streets of London there could be seen a few years ago, from five o'clock every morning until half past eight, a tidily set-out coffee-stall, consisting of a trestle and board, upon which stood two large tin cans, with a small fire of charcoal burning under each so as to keep the coffee boiling during the early hours of the morning when the work-people were thronging into the city on their way to their daily toil...

**Pages:84**
**Childrens** **ISBN:** *1-59462-373-2* *MSRP $9.95*

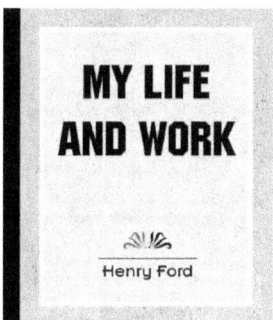

### My Life and Work
### Henry Ford

QTY

Henry Ford revolutionized the world with his implementation of mass production for the Model T automobile. Gain valuable business insight into his life and work with his own auto-biography... "We have only started on our development of our country we have not as yet, with all our talk of wonderful progress, done more than scratch the surface. The progress has been wonderful enough but..."

**Pages:300**
**Biographies/** **ISBN:** *1-59462-198-5* *MSRP $21.95*

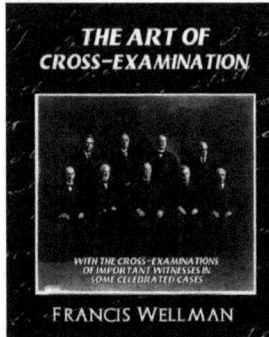

## The Art of Cross-Examination
## Francis Wellman

QTY

I presume it is the experience of every author, after his first book is published upon an important subject, to be almost overwhelmed with a wealth of ideas and illustrations which could readily have been included in his book, and which to his own mind, at least, seem to make a second edition inevitable. Such certainly was the case with me; and when the first edition had reached its sixth impression in five months, I rejoiced to learn that it seemed to my publishers that the book had met with a sufficiently favorable reception to justify a second and considerably enlarged edition. ..

**Pages:412**

Reference    ISBN: *1-59462-647-2*    *MSRP $19.95*

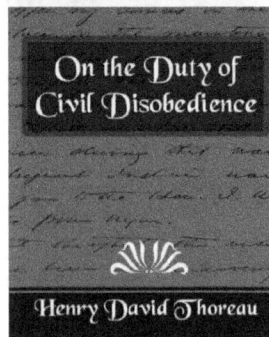

## On the Duty of Civil Disobedience
## Henry David Thoreau

QTY

Thoreau wrote his famous essay, On the Duty of Civil Disobedience, as a protest against an unjust but popular war and the immoral but popular institution of slave-owning. He did more than write—he declined to pay his taxes, and was hauled off to gaol in consequence. Who can say how much this refusal of his hastened the end of the war and of slavery ?

Law        ISBN: *1-59462-747-9*        **Pages:48**
*MSRP $7.45*

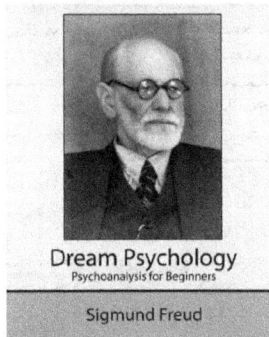

## Dream Psychology Psychoanalysis for Beginners
## Sigmund Freud

QTY

Sigmund Freud, born Sigismund Schlomo Freud (May 6, 1856 - September 23, 1939), was a Jewish-Austrian neurologist and psychiatrist who co-founded the psychoanalytic school of psychology. Freud is best known for his theories of the unconscious mind, especially involving the mechanism of repression; his redefinition of sexual desire as mobile and directed towards a wide variety of objects; and his therapeutic techniques, especially his understanding of transference in the therapeutic relationship and the presumed value of dreams as sources of insight into unconscious desires.

**Pages:196**

Psychology    ISBN: *1-59462-905-6*    *MSRP $15.45*

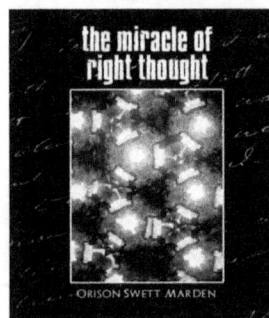

## The Miracle of Right Thought
## Orison Swett Marden

QTY

Believe with all of your heart that you will do what you were made to do. When the mind has once formed the habit of holding cheerful, happy, prosperous pictures, it will not be easy to form the opposite habit. It does not matter how improbable or how far away this realization may see, or how dark the prospects may be, if we visualize them as best we can, as vividly as possible, hold tenaciously to them and vigorously struggle to attain them, they will gradually become actualized, realized in the life. But a desire, a longing without endeavor, a yearning abandoned or held indifferently will vanish without realization.

**Pages:360**

Self Help        ISBN: *1-59462-644-8*        *MSRP $25.45*

**www.bookjungle.com** *email: sales@bookjungle.com fax: 630-214-0564 mail: Book Jungle PO Box 2226 Champaign, IL 61825*

QTY

☐ **The Rosicrucian Cosmo-Conception Mystic Christianity** *by Max Heindel*   ISBN: *1-59462-188-8*   **$38.95**
*The Rosicrucian Cosmo-conception is not dogmatic, neither does it appeal to any other authority than the reason of the student. It is: not controversial, but is: sent forth in the, hope that it may help to clear...*   *New Age/Religion Pages 646*

☐ **Abandonment To Divine Providence** *by Jean-Pierre de Caussade*   ISBN: *1-59462-228-0*   **$25.95**
*"The Rev. Jean Pierre de Caussade was one of the most remarkable spiritual writers of the Society of Jesus in France in the 18th Century. His death took place at Toulouse in 1751. His works have gone through many editions and have been republished...*   *Inspirational/Religion Pages 400*

☐ **Mental Chemistry** *by Charles Haanel*   ISBN: *1-59462-192-6*   **$23.95**
*Mental Chemistry allows the change of material conditions by combining and appropriately utilizing the power of the mind. Much like applied chemistry creates something new and unique out of careful combinations of chemicals the mastery of mental chemistry...*   *New Age Pages 354*

☐ **The Letters of Robert Browning and Elizabeth Barret Barrett 1845-1846 vol II**   ISBN: *1-59462-193-4*   **$35.95**
*by Robert Browning and Elizabeth Barrett*   *Biographies Pages 596*

☐ **Gleanings In Genesis (volume I)** *by Arthur W. Pink*   ISBN: *1-59462-130-6*   **$27.45**
*Appropriately has Genesis been termed "the seed plot of the Bible" for in it we have, in germ form, almost all of the great doctrines which are afterwards fully developed in the books of Scripture which follow...*   *Religion/Inspirational Pages 420*

☐ **The Master Key** *by L. W. de Laurence*   ISBN: *1-59462-001-6*   **$30.95**
*In no branch of human knowledge has there been a more lively increase of the spirit of research during the past few years than in the study of Psychology, Concentration and Mental Discipline. The requests for authentic lessons in Thought Control, Mental Discipline and...*   *New Age/Business Pages 422*

☐ **The Lesser Key Of Solomon Goetia** *by L. W. de Laurence*   ISBN: *1-59462-092-X*   **$9.95**
*This translation of the first book of the "Lemegton" which is now for the first time made accessible to students of Talismanic Magic was done, after careful collation and edition, from numerous Ancient Manuscripts in Hebrew, Latin, and French...*   *New Age/Occult Pages 92*

☐ **Rubaiyat Of Omar Khayyam** *by Edward Fitzgerald*   ISBN:*1-59462-332-5*   **$13.95**
*Edward Fitzgerald, whom the world has already learned, in spite of his own efforts to remain within the shadow of anonymity, to look upon as one of the rarest poets of the century, was born at Bredfield, in Suffolk, on the 31st of March, 1809. He was the third son of John Purcell...*   *Music Pages 172*

☐ **Ancient Law** *by Henry Maine*   ISBN: *1-59462-128-4*   **$29.95**
*The chief object of the following pages is to indicate some of the earliest ideas of mankind, as they are reflected in Ancient Law, and to point out the relation of those ideas to modern thought.*   *Religiom/History Pages 452*

☐ **Far-Away Stories** *by William J. Locke*   ISBN: *1-59462-129-2*   **$19.45**
*"Good wine needs no bush, but a collection of mixed vintages does. And this book is just such a collection. Some of the stories I do not want to remain buried for ever in the museum files of dead magazine-numbers an author's not unpardonable vanity..."*   *Fiction Pages 272*

☐ **Life of David Crockett** *by David Crockett*   ISBN: *1-59462-250-7*   **$27.45**
*"Colonel David Crockett was one of the most remarkable men of the times in which he lived. Born in humble life, but gifted with a strong will, an indomitable courage, and unremitting perseverance...*   *Biographies/New Age Pages 424*

☐ **Lip-Reading** *by Edward Nitchie*   ISBN: *1-59462-206-X*   **$25.95**
*Edward B. Nitchie, founder of the New York School for the Hard of Hearing, now the Nitchie School of Lip-Reading, Inc, wrote "LIP-READING Principles and Practice". The development and perfecting of this meritorious work on lip-reading was an undertaking...*   *How-to Pages 400*

☐ **A Handbook of Suggestive Therapeutics, Applied Hypnotism, Psychic Science**   ISBN: *1-59462-214-0*   **$24.95**
*by Henry Munro*   *Health/New Age/Health/Self-help Pages 376*

☐ **A Doll's House: and Two Other Plays** *by Henrik Ibsen*   ISBN: *1-59462-112-8*   **$19.95**
*Henrik Ibsen created this classic when in revolutionary 1848 Rome. Introducing some striking concepts in playwriting for the realist genre, this play has been studied the world over.*   *Fiction/Classics/Plays 308*

☐ **The Light of Asia** *by sir Edwin Arnold*   ISBN: *1-59462-204-3*   **$13.95**
*In this poetic masterpiece, Edwin Arnold describes the life and teachings of Buddha. The man who was to become known as Buddha to the world was born as Prince Gautama of India but he rejected the worldly riches and abandoned the reigns of power when...*   *Religion/History/Biographies Pages 170*

☐ **The Complete Works of Guy de Maupassant** *by Guy de Maupassant*   ISBN: *1-59462-157-8*   **$16.95**
*"For days and days, nights and nights, I had dreamed of that first kiss which was to consecrate our engagement, and I knew not on what spot I should put my lips..."*   *Fiction/Classics Pages 240*

☐ **The Art of Cross-Examination** *by Francis L. Wellman*   ISBN: *1-59462-309-0*   **$26.95**
*Written by a renowned trial lawyer, Wellman imparts his experience and uses case studies to explain how to use psychology to extract desired information through questioning.*   *How-to/Science/Reference Pages 408*

☐ **Answered or Unanswered?** *by Louisa Vaughan*   ISBN: *1-59462-248-5*   **$10.95**
*Miracles of Faith in China*   *Religion Pages 112*

☐ **The Edinburgh Lectures on Mental Science (1909)** *by Thomas*   ISBN: *1-59462-008-3*   **$11.95**
*This book contains the substance of a course of lectures recently given by the writer in the Queen Street Hall, Edinburgh. Its purpose is to indicate the Natural Principles governing the relation between Mental Action and Material Conditions...*   *New Age/Psychology Pages 148*

☐ **Ayesha** *by H. Rider Haggard*   ISBN: *1-59462-301-5*   **$24.95**
*Verily and indeed it is the unexpected that happens! Probably if there was one person upon the earth from whom the Editor of this, and of a certain previous history, did not expect to hear again...*   *Classics Pages 380*

☐ **Ayala's Angel** *by Anthony Trollope*   ISBN: *1-59462-352-X*   **$29.95**
*The two girls were both pretty, but Lucy who was twenty-one who supposed to be simple and comparatively unattractive, whereas Ayala was credited, as her Bombwhat romantic name might show, with poetic charm and a taste for romance. Ayala when her father died was nineteen...*   *Fiction Pages 484*

☐ **The American Commonwealth** *by James Bryce*   ISBN: *1-59462-286-8*   **$34.45**
*An interpretation of American democratic political theory. It examines political mechanics and society from the perspective of Scotsman James Bryce*   *Politics Pages 572*

☐ **Stories of the Pilgrims** *by Margaret P. Pumphrey*   ISBN: *1-59462-116-0*   **$17.95**
*This book explores pilgrims religious oppression in England as well as their escape to Holland and eventual crossing to America on the Mayflower, and their early days in New England...*   *History Pages 268*

QTY

**The Fasting Cure** *by Sinclair Upton*                                          ISBN: *1-59462-222-1*  **$13.95**
*In the Cosmopolitan Magazine for May, 1910, and in the Contemporary Review (London) for April, 1910, I published an article dealing with my experiences in fasting. I have written a great many magazine articles, but never one which attracted so much attention...* New Age/Self Help/Health Pages 164

**Hebrew Astrology** *by Sepharial*                                          ISBN: *1-59462-308-2*  **$13.45**
*In these days of advanced thinking it is a matter of common observation that we have left many of the old landmarks behind and that we are now pressing forward to greater heights and to a wider horizon than that which represented the mind-content of our progenitors...*  Astrology Pages 144

**Thought Vibration or The Law of Attraction in the Thought World**            ISBN: *1-59462-127-6*  **$12.95**
*by William Walker Atkinson*                                                    Psychology/Religion Pages 144

**Optimism** *by Helen Keller*                                               ISBN: *1-59462-108-X*  **$15.95**
*Helen Keller was blind, deaf, and mute since 19 months old, yet famously learned how to overcome these handicaps, communicate with the world, and spread her lectures promoting optimism. An inspiring read for everyone...*  Biographies/Inspirational Pages 84

**Sara Crewe** *by Frances Burnett*                                           ISBN: *1-59462-360-0*  **$9.45**
*In the first place, Miss Minchin lived in London. Her home was a large, dull, tall one, in a large, dull square, where all the houses were alike, and all the sparrows were alike, and where all the door-knockers made the same heavy sound...*  Childrens/Classic Pages 88

**The Autobiography of Benjamin Franklin** *by Benjamin Franklin*             ISBN: *1-59462-135-7*  **$24.95**
*The Autobiography of Benjamin Franklin has probably been more extensively read than any other American historical work, and no other book of its kind has had such ups and downs of fortune. Franklin lived for many years in England, where he was agent...*  Biographies/History Pages 332

| | |
|---|---|
| **Name** | |
| **Email** | |
| **Telephone** | |
| **Address** | |
| | |
| **City, State ZIP** | |

☐ **Credit Card**        ☐ **Check / Money Order**

| | |
|---|---|
| **Credit Card Number** | |
| **Expiration Date** | |
| **Signature** | |

*Please Mail to:*  Book Jungle
                    PO Box 2226
                    Champaign, IL 61825
*or Fax to:*        630-214-0564

## ORDERING INFORMATION

**web***: www.bookjungle.com*
**email***: sales@bookjungle.com*
**fax***: 630-214-0564*
**mail***: Book Jungle PO Box 2226 Champaign, IL 61825*
**or PayPal** *to sales@bookjungle.com*

*Please contact us for bulk discounts*

## DIRECT-ORDER TERMS

**20% Discount if You Order
Two or More Books**
Free Domestic Shipping!
Accepted: Master Card, Visa,
Discover, American Express

www.ingramcontent.com/pod-product-compliance
Lightning Source LLC
LaVergne TN
LVHW081325060426
835511LV00011B/1861